Mobilizing for Human Rights
in Latin America

Mobilizing for Human Rights in Latin America

Edward Cleary

Kumarian
Press, Inc.

Mobilizing for Human Rights in Latin America

Published 2007 in the United States of America by Kumarian Press, Inc.
1294 Blue Hills Avenue, Bloomfield, CT 06002 USA

Copyright © 2007 Kumarian Press. All rights reserved.

No part of this book may be reproduced or transmitted in any form or by any means, electronic or mechanical, including photocopy, recording, or information storage and retrieval system, without prior permission of the publisher.

For permission to photocopy or use material electronically from *Mobilizing for Human Rights in Latin America* please access www.copyright.com or contact Copyright Clearance Center, Inc. (CCC), 222 Rosewood Drive, Danvers, MA 01923, 978-750-8400. CCC is a not-for-profit organization that provides licenses and registration for a variety of users.

Copyedit by Claire Slagle
Proofread by Beth Richards
Design and production by UB Communications, Parsippany, NJ.
The text of this book is set in 10.5/13 Bulmer.

Printed in the USA on acid-free paper by Thomson-Shore, Inc.

♾ The paper used in this publication meets the minimum requirements of the American National Standard for Information Sciences—Permanence of Paper for Printed Library Materials, ANSI Z39.48-1984.

Library of Congress Cataloging-in-Publication Data

Cleary, Edward L.
    Mobilizing for human rights in Latin America / by Edward L. Cleary.
      p. cm.
    Includes bibliographical references and index.
    ISBN 978-1-56549-241-7 (pbk. : alk. paper) — ISBN 978-1-56549-242-4 (cloth : alk. paper)
1. Human rights movements—Latin America. I. Title.
    JC599.L3C57 2007
    323.098—dc22
                          2007026229

Contents

Acknowledgments

From Chiloé through Santiago to Tegucigalpa and Mexico City, the debts incurred in gathering data and oral histories for this volume over a seven-year period have been extensive. The author began with a general outline of a picture of human rights in the new millennium that gradually became clearer. Elizabeth Lira, Diego Irarrázaval, Monseñor Sergio Valech, Daniel Flynn, Robert Pelton, Juan Pablo Corsiglio, and Miguel Concha each helped to shape this vision. The resulting Latin American panorama brought some positive surprises, such as the gains made by women, and some puzzling omissions, such as the primitive state of the rights of the disabled. My appreciation of the disabled grew during the writing of this book when I suffered a debilitating stroke. Colleen Fitzsimmons, Dr. Alice Barton, and a team of therapists breathed new life into me.

Participation in a seminar on human rights conducted by Beatriz Manz at the University of California, Berkeley, served as a spark for moving beyond transitional justice, as did my research assistants, especially Dan Menendez and Paul Fusaro who argued that I was too interested in the past. My colleagues in political science at Providence College, especially Bob Trudeau and Paola Cesarini, supported me in extraordinary ways. Faculty grants from Providence College made research and networking possible, and my brother David Orique reinforced the pleasure of research as a discovery process. To all, my profound gratitude.

Introduction

A New Era
in Human Rights Mobilization
in Latin America

The watershed event in the contemporary human rights period for most observers who followed Latin America from the United States and Europe was the bloody coup that occurred on the "other September 11th."[1] On that date in 1973, Chile's four security branches, under the leadership of General Augusto Pinochet Urgarte, took over the government from a legally elected president, a Marxist-socialist, Salvador Allende Gossens.

Human rights organizing gained world attention for Latin America in the 1970s and 1980s. Military governments took over most countries in South and Central America. State repressive measures typically followed. In Mexico, one-party rule controlled the country from 1929 to 2000, often through authoritarian and arbitrary measures.

What follows is a brief account of a period in which human rights organizing became a social and political movement and serves as an essential background for understanding the wide variety of human rights issues being pursued at the end of the first decade of the twenty-first century. As will be seen, human rights activism flourished under very difficult circumstances but brought forth significant gains.

The center of attention of this volume tilts as well toward the persons and groups organizing for human rights protection as on the issues themselves; that is, on mobilizations for human rights. The major change within Latin American society of interest to long-time observers of Latin America is active response from the grassroots and middle levels of societies. Latin America, to the surprise of many, became a movement society, one in which movements concerned about various issues appeared, many of them focused on human rights. These movements, generally speaking, were aimed at improving the shape of the world in which Latin Americans lived. This was a major shift away from passivity and fatalism toward empowerment or agency. Previous attitudes of dependency were related to government and to ruling elites. They became transformed to a more self-reliant outlook. This transformation was a sea change.

These changes also served as the foundation of a strong civil society. Indeed, Latin America has, estimates say, more than one million civil society organizations.

This shift occurred under great pressure and no small suffering. In Chile, the military government blanketed the country with security measures that amounted to state-sponsored terrorism. Through the infamous Caravan of Death and other repressive operations, military and police put down any armed resistance.[2] But they also indiscriminately killed, disappeared (a new tactic), imprisoned, and tortured thousands of citizens and some foreigners who were suspected but not tried for opposition to the new government. Because Chile had been a showcase for democracy, with a strong political party system, respect for the rule of law, and a highly-developed sense of citizenship, the change to military rule became a rude and unwelcome shock to Chileans and their supporters who had trusted in democratic rule.

Chile, as well as much of Latin America in the 1970s, was in the throes of the worst aspects of the Cold War. Latin American militaries, without consent of the general public, constructed a Doctrine of National Security. This led them to believe that Marxists and communists were determined to take over the region. Guarding against subversion became the focus for security forces. The fears of communist takeover were heightened by events at Latin America's own doorstep. By the early 1960s, Cuba had succumbed to guerrilla forces that turned the large-island state into a communist showcase with resources from the Soviet Union and an avowed determination to export their revolution.

This communist influence was to be stopped at all costs. The costs for society were high and varied from country to country. In terms of numbers killed, Guatemala, with 200,000 dead, was the worst and indeed approached the level of ethnocide, since most of the dead were indigenous. Argentina was second with some 30,000 killed. Most of the killing in Argentina affected persons in urban areas over a two-year period, so what happened in Argentina seemed especially stultifying. Chile had some 3,300 killed, mostly by the military, and a few hundred official forces were killed by guerrillas. Uruguay had a very large percentage of its population terrorized by torture or imprisonment but not many killed. Brazil's military killed fewer than two hundred; but, in a situation similar to that in Uruguay, the military terrorized sectors of its population through harassment, torture, and imprisonment. Other countries were less notable in the negative effects of military rule. Mexico's one-party authoritarian rulers efficiently stifled opposition through a "dirty war" that still lacks official accounting.

Chileans began organizing quickly and as best they could under government control. Churches were the only institutions with a measure of freedom in society, so these were used as focal points for human rights advocacy. Lay persons and clerics created the Committee for Peace. When the forces of the dictator Pinochet tried to limit the Committee for Peace, Cardinal Raul Silva Henríquez of Santiago took the organization under his wing and created the Vicariate for Solidarity. The Vicariate became an icon of human rights organizing and resistance to repression.

Reactions to the Chilean military takeover in Washington, New York, and European capitals was very rapid. Organizing in overseas countries in order to do something about the injustices in Chile soon extended itself to other Latin American countries, as these also fell under repressive rule. The human rights era of Latin America had begun.

A transnational human rights movement started on both sides of the Rio Grande. The larger phenomenon we call a social or political movement was forming: that is, a network of groups pulled together to promote common demands on the state. Very few human rights groups existed in Latin America before the military era. The few that did exist were generally concerned with labor rights and had a leftist orientation.

Human rights—translated as *derechos humanos* in Spanish or *direitos humanos* in Portuguese—were not unknown in Latin America before military takeovers. However, the term seemed new to many advocates who claimed to have heard the phrase in common usage, say, only in 1975. But a select group of Latin Americans, working within the budding Inter-American system that eventually became the Organization of American States, had worked on and composed a Declaration of the Rights of Man as early as the 1930s, and women were objecting to the use of rights of "man" as early as the 1940s. There is, in fact, a long historical tradition of human rights in Latin America, a theme that is developed in the first chapter.

Human rights in the 1970s and 1980s meant struggling against death and disappearance, arbitrary arrest, torture and inhuman imprisonment. Other issues, such as political, social, and economic rights, would have to take a lower priority to issues of life and death. Among those urgent issues, disappearance was a relatively new and acutely cruel practice. Suspected dissidents were picked up in their homes or on the streets and never seen again. Their bodies were buried in unmarked graves or, not uncommonly, dropped in the ocean. Friends and relatives spent lifetimes wondering what happened to their loved ones and never having the emotional release of burying their dead.

The human rights movement in Latin America contributed to a turn toward democracy while under military or authoritarian rule. This push was called the Third Wave of Democratization by Samuel Huntington of Harvard and included most of Latin America, except Cuba and perhaps Haiti, which has nearly become a collapsed state. Democracy was forthcoming, in part because attention to human rights created a strong impetus for citizen participation and the rule of law, major components of democracy.

The turn to democracy brought two streams of activity for human rights advocates. First was dealing with the past. This became an all-consuming task for many persons. Indeed, the impulse seemed to be exaggerated for many observers from the Old World. Europe dealt with its past mostly by pacts of silence and tacit agreements not to stir things up. Spain and many other countries did not deal in a significant way in either clarifying for the historical record what took place in terms of death or inhuman treatment or in holding agents responsible for past misconduct. Europeans got on with their lives. Latin Americans chose not to. Therein lies a notable difference, one worth examination in the next chapter.

Dealing with its past took various forms in Latin America, from modest to magnanimous. All the countries did something to settle with the past, except Uruguay. Most efforts were limited for several reasons: the military felt they were justified in their past actions; the military had the potential for armed violence to stop the proceedings; legislators were timid; various other reasons were alleged, including the need to get on with one's life. By most accounts, even limited efforts were worth the pain of reawakened memories and sometimes dangerous efforts. Bishop Juan Girardi, head of one of the three Guatemalan truth commissions, was clubbed to death two days after he delivered the church's four-volume report called *Guatemala: Never Again*.[3] In one way or another, these efforts brought closure to the past and restored a measure of justice to society.

Efforts to deal with the past seemed to be never-ending until recently. Chile mounted a major effort to settle the past with the Rettig Commission Report in 1991, a year after the military left power. Six years later, when Chile was settling down to times of relative prosperity and social peace, memories of torture and unjust imprisonment erupted as unsettled questions, as is noted in Chapter 7. Chile took a second major step to address its past in forming the Valech Commission, known officially as the National Commission on Political Prison and Torture, which reported its findings in 2004–2005. That Commission represents what may be the last effort in Latin America to deal with the past. Most persons who ordered or committed past crimes have died or are about ready to die of natural causes or their memories have atrophied through old age.

The impressive compiling of what took place through historical clarification or truth and justice commissions (the names and purposes of commissions vary from country to country) now fills many shelves of archives, scholars' offices, and high school inspirational reading sections. Notable monuments, such as Villa Grimaldi in Santiago or the filmed depiction of the destruction of Caseros prison in Buenos Aires, will also remain, along with such classic films as *Missing*, *Official Story*, and *Romero*, as testaments to the period.

Dealing with the past has become an academic subfield, called transitional justice, within the study of human rights. Practitioners in that field have developed increasing sophistication in theory and have extended their efforts to greater comparative understanding through inclusion of regions other than Latin America. Thus, we leave the treatment of past offenses to explore what human rights violations Latin Americans now select for attention and for mobilization.

The energies generated by reactions to human rights violations during the military era have flowed into a second stream of mobilizations. Human rights advocacy has expanded into areas beyond death and disappearance. What these themes are, why these arose as priorities, what is being done, and what accomplishments have been made form the substance of the chapters to follow.

The choices of themes for this volume were thus made by Latin Americans and are indicated by the priorities of their human rights organizations. One might regret, as does the author, that some rights, such as the rights of the disabled, are not well emphasized, but Latin American human rights advocates have an abundance of worthy targets and will need all the resolve they can summon to attack their choices, as we shall see.

NOTES

1. James N. Green, *We Cannot Remain Silent: Opposition to the Brazilian Military Dictatorship in the United States*, 1964–1985, forthcoming.

2. For a vivid look at the inner workings of the Chilean military, see Patricia Verdugo, *Chile, Pinochet, and the Caravan of Death* (Miami, FL: University of Miami Press, 2001).

3. *Guatemala Never Again* was published in English by Orbis Books in 1999.

Mobilizing for Human Rights
in Latin America

1

Is There a Distinctive Tradition of Human Rights in Latin America?

The Universal Declaration is the essential document.
—Nadine Gordimer, Nobel laureate[1]

The Declaration played an extraordinary role in the history of mankind.
—José Lingren Alves[2]

When Hernán Santa Cruz Barceló, a relatively unknown Chilean jurist and academic, participated in the first meeting of the United Nations General Assembly in 1946, he began to take his place in history. Over the next months he served as one of the main contributors to the writing of the Universal Declaration of Human Rights.

That he and other Latin Americans played major roles in the establishment of the United Nations as a major instrument for human rights promotion would come as a surprise to most inexperienced observers who were accustomed to viewing Latin America as an object of humans rights concern rather than an active subject. The view expressed here is that Latin America has had a distinctive human rights tradition. It is a tradition worth study since it balances deficiencies in both North American and European rights traditions. This tradition placed Latin Americans in a position whereby they contributed both to the creation of the United Nations and to the Universal Declaration of Human Rights.

We begin with this tradition because it furnishes three sets of influences that have affected Latin American society and politics. These are Christian humanism of Las Casas and early missionaries, secular influences of the Enlightenment modified by Latin Americans, and the political influences of the United States constitution.

To many who have lived in Latin America and followed their human rights situation for some years, there is something special about Latin America and human rights. There is a zeal-zeitgeist-soul to human rights advocates and discussions that one does not commonly find in the United States, Canada, or Europe. In interviewing Elizabeth Jelin in Argentina, Elizabeth Lira in Chile, Luis Pérez Aguirre in Uruguay, or Bishop

Juan Girardi in Guatemala, one acquired a sense that the door does not close on the past and that progression in human rights never ends. More, human rights language is embedded in the intellectual history of Latin America.

Why is it that every country that suffered state repression in Latin America has done something about its past while no other region has done so? Why have Latin American women made more progress in some areas, as women national legislators, than women from many other regions including the United States and southern Europe, if not for this tradition?

The following sections address, first, Latin American participation in the founding of the United Nations and the Universal Declaration of Human Rights. The second section takes up the Latin American views of key Enlightenment themes in human rights and modern constitutions. The final section deals with twentieth-century human rights initiatives.

FOUNDING OF UNITED NATIONS AND
THE UNIVERSAL DECLARATION

An appropriate place to begin, as Mary Ann Glendon of Harvard Law School and Paolo Carozzo of Notre Dame Law School have done in tracing the Latin American human rights tradition[3] is with the history of how the United Nations and its key document, the Universal Declaration of Human Rights, came into being. Their research and that of several other scholars, including Johannes Morsink,[4] help to highlight the contributions of Latin America to both events. The telling of this history was obscured by many writers who emphasized the tensions between the United States-Northern Europe and the Soviet bloc in the creation of the United Nations. Once the Cold War waned, younger scholars began reading memoirs of key actors, perusing archived documents, and reconstructing the foundational events.

From that scholarship it became clear that emphasis on human rights as a purpose of the United Nations and the existence of the Universal Declaration were in a discernible measure due to Latin America.[5] That the United States, France, and Britain in 1945 were cool and the Communist countries hostile to emphasis on human rights at the United Nations is incontestable. The United States at that time actively practiced racial segregation and inequality; France and Britain still had colonial empires. The Communists repressed their subjects as a routine practice. Latin America had a human rights tradition, as will be shown, but it also had more on its mind: the propensity of the United States to intrude on the sovereignty of its neighbors. Panama had what it considered its prime resource, the Canal, under the control of the United States.

At the founding of the United Nations at San Francisco in 1945, Latin America was the largest single group with twenty countries among fifty-six nations. The agenda was fairly well set at a prior meeting by larger powers at Dumbarton Oaks. Smaller powers

Las Casas and others obtained from Charles V the New Laws that did away with aspects of the latifundium but continued in practice as encomienda. This was hardly a victory, as the landless in Brazil and elsewhere in Latin America can attest, but Las Casas brought forward ideas that would eventually have consequences.

If anything is key and important about Las Casas it is that rights are universal. They are not just for Europeans. Further, he condemned slavery.[15] Equal in importance—and sometimes overlooked—Las Casas believed that all persons are endowed with freedom. He wrote *The Only Way of Attracting People to the True Religion* is persuasion, not coercion. When asked if Spaniards should go to war to stop some Indians from human sacrifice, he did not think so.

Las Casas believed in cultural integrity. He argued for the need to understand behavior and values of native peoples. Four hundred years later, an indigenous theology was emerging.[16] Above all for the argument here, since Las Casas's death, a continuous discourse has taken place in Latin America about dignity, rights, and freedom. Theologian José Comblin argued that current human rights issues derive from that five-hundred-year-old experience. "The challenge for the church and for Christianity was raised by these events; we do not speak about human rights because the idea sprung from the mind of some philosophers, but because it was inscribed in history by the sacrificial struggle of prophets who knew how to stand up to the spontaneous tendencies of the majority of their contemporaries."[17]

Dignity, the author believes, exists in many, perhaps most, Latin Americans' persona and is distinctive. Ordinary people carry themselves as persons worth of dignity, whether or not they have earned it by money or achievements. They have it by the simple fact of being human beings and they believe that. When unschooled Latin American friends, kitchen workers, and mechanics talk to the author, they think of themselves as equals as persons, expecting to be heard and respected for their views on politics, religion, and other topics.

Las Casas's ideas entered Latin American tradition. In the early nineteenth century these ideas were well known and cited by Simón Bolívar. He referred to Las Casas as "a humane hero." He wanted to name the new capital city of his proposed Pan American Union after Las Casas.[18]

LATIN AMERICAN INTERPRETATION OF THE ENLIGHTENMENT AND MODERN CONSTITUTIONS

A great wellspring for human rights, the Enlightenment had a different understanding in Latin America than it did in France. Neither popular sovereignty nor anticlericalism had the same place or meaning. The separation from Spain that was about to take place when independence was achieved in 1810–1825 was not a revolution to compare with France's. More or less, the same social and economic order continued.

Ideas parallel to those of France were nonetheless common. It was commonplace in universities to teach on the priority of natural law over written law, the legitimacy of resistance to tyranny and unjust laws, and existence of certain rights and guarantees by reason of one's humanity. Other venues for this discussion were *tertulias* and literary Sunday supplements that were common features of civil society. No surprise, then, that as rebellion approached, the Spanish crown tried to do away with professorships of public law, natural law, and jus gentium in colonial schools.

Although modified, Enlightenment ideas did fall on fertile soil and were absorbed. The French Declaration of Rights of Man grew in Latin America within the inherited traditions of thought. Mexican writer Silvio Zavala says: "Independence and liberalism were in accord with a caste of mind that long existed an enduring desire for justice and freedom that led us to venerate, among others, the fighting figure of Las Casas." José Martí, the great Cuban patriot of the late nineteenth century, summoned "Padre Las Casas" as a familiar figure in Latin American consciousness and source of ideas that would serve Cubans well.[19]

The US constitutional ideas also acted as major influences. All three streams of ideas were reflected in the constitutions of new republics. Thus, these constitutions differ from that of the United States and its Bill of Rights. As Paolo Carozzo noted, the US Bill of Rights has few, terse, and restrained injunctions, as Congress shall make no law abridging the freedom of speech. By contrast, the Colombian Constitution states the "first obligation of the citizen aims at the preservation of society and thus requires that those who constitute it know and fulfill their respective duties." Further, "No one is a good citizen who is not also a good son, a good father, a good brother, a good friend, a good husband."

A later round of constitutions began in Latin America after the 1910 Mexican Revolution. The Mexican Constitution of 1917 was the first of any constitutional document in the world to incorporate social and economic guarantees and protections in addition to classical civil and political liberties. Mexican schoolboys and girls read and frequently memorize Articles 23 and 123. Article 23 describes aspects of the social function of property. It provides that the Nation shall have at times the right to impose on private property such limitations as the public interest may demand, including necessary measures to divide large landed estates. Article 123 treats labor rights and working conditions, such as maximum hours, child labor, laborers' health and safety, the right to organize and strike, establishment of pensions, and unemployment and accident insurance. The provisions could fill a book.

These and similar articles were later incorporated into constitutions in Latin America and elsewhere. The Mexican Constitution went beyond individual rights, adding solicitude for social concerns and solidarity with the working class. The writers of the Constitution drew from experience of the Revolution and from tradition. One of the writers was a Catholic presumed to know *Rerum Novarum*, the first modern document of the social teaching of the Catholic Church.

TWENTIETH-CENTURY HUMAN RIGHTS INITIATIVES

From the 1930s, the American states began to band together in new ways. The American states met in 1933 to discuss rights and duties of states. This was followed by the 1938 Inter-American Conference that created the Declaration in Defense of Human Rights. The conference also passed resolutions on racial and religious persecution, women's rights, and the right of association for workers.

During this period a revival of scholarly interest in Las Casas and his ideas occurred, first in the Spanish-speaking world, and then in the United States. The authors of the two widely used textbooks on Latin American history,[20] Benjamin Keen and Lewis Hanke, one blacklisted by McCarthy witch-hunters and the other a consummate New England Protestant scholar, both devoted many of their best years to making Las Casas known.[21] There should be no question then that Latin Americans were ready to contribute to the Universal Declaration. Further, they had help from sectors in the United States. The American Law Institute there furnished arguments for human rights formulations that Panama put forward at the United Nations. No wonder, then, that this nation of then barely a million persons could put forward arguments that proved persuasive to many other delegates.

The Latin American women active in the early days of the United Nations also came from a history of women organizing and expressing their ideas. In the following chapter, we note accomplishments of contemporary Latin American women in such other areas as political participation. Behind the efforts of Minerva Bernardino and Bertha Lutz at the United Nations and current gains for women were important milestones. In 1923, the Fifth Pan American Congress resolved that all its programs would work to abolish all laws and decrees that hindered women's rights. At the 1928 Congress women made a breakthrough. They demanded to be heard through months of protest and finally received a voice in what would become the Organization of American States (OAS). At the meeting held in Havana, women officially spoke for the first time. More than a thousand women listened, filling the galleries, hallways, and conference floor of the University of Havana's Great Hall. Here was clear evidence of the emerging women's movements in the region. In the same year, the organization created the Inter-American Women's Commission. This was followed by the Convention on the Nationality of Married Women in 1938 and Conventions on Women's Political and Civil Rights in 1948.

After its promulgation, the Universal Declaration served Latin Americans well, as did its own human rights tradition. One of the clearest cases of this tradition coming alive is Chiapas, Mexico. Chiapas would become world renowned for its uprising in January 1994 to protest the signing of the North American Free Trade Agreement, but behind the scenes and largely apart from the armed Zapatistas of the uprising, a large nonviolent movement among the indigenous was taking place. When the governor of the state of Chiapas ordered the First Congress of Indigenous People in 1974, the event was the first opportunity in 500 years for four ethnic groups to unite and to discuss their situation in public, a privilege previously reserved to mestizos. Christine Kovic called the event a "watershed in political mobilization."[22] The governor called for the congress as a way to commemorate the five hundredth anniversary of the first bishop, Bartolomé de Las Casas. Organizers and participants took a year to prepare for the congress, thereby laying the groundwork for the activism that followed. The year of meeting at various levels focused on describing the situation of indigenous communities and reflecting on Las Casas's work in relation to human rights. Thus, they recalled the policies and practices of the original bishop of Chiapas, Las Casas.[23]

Some 1,200 delegates from 327 communities took part in the congress. To continue the work of the congress an organization named Fray Bartolomé de Las Casas was created and helped to imbue a new spirit in the communities. Three years later one of the advisers to the organization asked: "Who will be the new Bartolomé de Las Casas?" The bishop recalls that the indigenous people answered: "We will. We are Bartolomé. We needed one before because everything was decided in Spain, where we couldn't go and where we didn't have voice; then they spoke for us. Now we are beginning to speak for ourselves."[24]

The event served as a catalyst for change in the region and for further transformation in the bishop. Many observers noted the change in the resident bishop, Samuel Ruiz García, from conservative pastor who set out in 1960 to Christianize the natives to a leader who began to listen to the indigenous and to understand their oppression and the rights denied them for centuries. Ruiz also acted as a mediator between government and people. The script written by Las Casas was being followed 500 years later.

A strong sense of the religious mobilization of dissent among the Mayan indigenous can be seen in Nash's work[25] and in Danielle Bible's *The Catholic Church in Chiapas; Empowered, Relentless, and a Threat to the PRI.*[26] Women especially benefited from the empowerment that took place in San Cristóbal de Las Casas and in other areas of Chiapas. Christine Eber and Christine Kovic, both former students of June Nash, gathered evidence in their *Women of Chiapas* of the growing awareness of inequalities faced by women, as well as their determination to work together to improve the living conditions of their communities (again the communitarian spirit noted by Las Casas and differing from the Enlightenment), as well as seeking gender equity and social justice. Kovic believed that the women demanded their dignity as daughters of God, seeking human rights as Catholic women.

Kovic further elaborates not only the protection afforded by the church but the internalization of human rights language in *Mayan Voices for Human Rights* (2005). When objects of human rights advocacy become subjects of their own empowerment and agency, a dream begun centuries earlier was being realized.

The Cold War, authoritarianism, and other factors brought a period of great repression to many Latin American nations. Even after military or authoritarian regimes left the presidential palace, the region was left with legacies of authoritarian rule, as noted in other chapters, in practices of policing, including torture; and the growing presence of street children and of the landless. In both situations Latin Americans had the benefit of having the Universal Declaration in place and recognized as a global standard of governmental behavior and a way to put things right. Further, the heroic efforts put forward by Argentines, Chileans, and others in the darkest days of oppression were, as Carozzo said, reminders of a modern-day Las Casas and a living tradition.[27]

CONCLUSION

It has been argued here that Latin Americans have been more than objects of the attention of human rights advocates. They have been active and creative in human rights protection. This became clearest at the beginning of the United Nations when the twenty-nation Latin American bloc helped design the organization. As the United Nations says of itself: "There are few causes with which the United Nations is more closely associated than the promotion and protection of human rights." The Universal Declaration of Human Rights was pushed forward and carried to completion especially by Latin Americans. The Declaration reflects not only contemporary efforts but a long and distinctive tradition within Latin America. This tradition bears the marks not only of Las Casas and Bolívar but also the language of justice and freedom that thousands of ordinary citizens learned to speak and to cherish. Human rights discourse is a language Latin Americans participate in by birthright.

Should this language in global circles become impoverished, as Mary Ann Glendon believes it has,[28] Latin Americans may have more work to do in the future, but this effort would not be new. For any tradition to continue it has to be reformulated, adapted, and in some aspects changed.

Change—that is, adaptation not accommodation—has been true of five hundred years of resistance by Latin America's indigenous. Their cultures have not been so much preserved as recreated and reshaped to fit into one or another age. In doing so, the indigenous have found a resurgent voice.[29] Las Casas saw something in the Indians that many others did not see. If there is something special about Latin America's tradition of human rights, it may be due in part to encounters with indigenous cultures that have emphasized a utopian view of justice and of making thing right. The Spanish (following the Romans) added to this, bringing a measure of justice to earth through laws. Further, the Enlightenment and the US Constitution offered not only laws but the rule of law as the practical norm that may be the last great building block for the relatively new Latin American democracies.

Further, given modernist tendencies in a globalized world, the metaphysical and ethical views of natural rights cherished by Latin Americans may have to give way to arguments from language and practicality. In a postmodernist vein, Michael Ignatieff has argued: "Rights language says: all human beings belong at the table, in the essential conversation of how we should treat each other." Latin Americans would agree. More, the language of human rights is one that Latin Americans have been speaking for a long time. José Lindgren suggests that in a postmodernist world the Declaration may be the Grand Narrative. If so, Latin Americans have been masters of narratives, small and large, magical and real.[30]

In sum, one may doubt that the United Nations would have concentrated on human rights from the beginning of its history without the strong advocacy of Latin America, in contrast to the coolness of the United States, France, and Britain and the hostility of the Communist bloc. The Universal Declaration of Human Rights stands as a major achievement, one to which Latin Americans contributed to and benefit from. It represents a major milestone in a long tradition of human rights now shared within a framework of global solidarity.

NEW VOICES IN HUMAN RIGHTS

The three influences of the Latin American human rights tradition—Christian humanism from Las Casas et al., Enlightenment ideas modified by Latin Americans, and modern constitutionalism—became embodied in the Organization of American States and then in the Universal Declaration. This tradition was being kept alive among legal scholars and the lettered class. These thoughtful Latin Americans wrote for the Sunday literary supplements and kept ideas alive in tertulias throughout the region. Also, as noted, by the 1950s renewed interest in Las Casas occurred.

However, widespread thirst for justice and human rights in Latin America occurred only when justice and rights were threatened on a massive scale by state-sponsored repression by the military or authoritarian governments. The energies generated by reactions to injustices flowed into the wave of democratization that occurred in Latin America in the 1970s through the early 1990s. Fair and clean elections followed, but Latin Americans demanded more than electoral democracies, formal democracies that appeared to some observers to be only shell democracies.

Something new had occurred among many Latin Americans. They demanded a new relationship with their politicians. A more sophisticated and demanding citizenry, as Enrique Peruzzotti and others have noted, emerged from battles with an oppressive state and the fight for the rule of law. Further, human rights discourse gained legitimacy in the public arena. It became a common language for conducting public affairs. Human rights became a priority issue for many political parties in the region.

A sense exists in which Latin Americans are living in a post-human rights era, that is, citizens of the region have advanced beyond issues of death and disappearance to face new concerns, as rights for women, children, landless and other issues covered herein. New voices have emerged to make spaces for rights long ignored within Latin American societies.

This democratization after authoritarian rule is not a return to a democratic past. For most countries a full-fledged democracy never existed. Brazil was said to be one of the democracies that fought the Fascist Germans and Italians in World War II, but Brazil was democratic only in some formalities. Even countries with democratic pasts, such as Chile, Costa Rica, and Uruguay, are different today, as are Latin American countries generally. This difference derives largely from two developments in the region: first, the flourishing of nongovernmental organizations and civic associations. Then, a new inquisitive journalism has taken root in most countries: media that act as watchdogs instead of lapdogs of elected authorities and appointed administrators. Together the two sectors force politicians into a new type of politics, that of rights and accountability.

Thus, groups promoting citizens' rights have opened up a wide field of rights that we shall shortly explore. They operate in a changed environment. Political leaders no longer have a "blank check." Once it was enough to be elected for strong or charismatic leaders to say to voters: trust me. Victor Paz Esstensoro in Bolivia, Daniel Ortega in 1980s Nicaragua—above all, Juan Peron and Getulio Vargas—and dozen of other leaders thought they knew what was best and went ahead with projects and policies as if delegated to act without scrutiny. Now elected officials are monitored and controlled. Citizens, organizations, and media contest decisions and condemn the unlawful actions of public officials. The mechanisms of vertical and horizontal accountability are in place. This has produced a newer and deeper type of democracy. Peruzzotti notes: "Working safeguards against unresponsive or irresponsible behavior on the part of officials generates trust in institutions."[31]

Citizens and media pressuring for accountability have taken a high toll on Latin American presidents. The first president to be impeached in Latin American history was Fernando Collor de Mello of Brazil in the 1980s, followed by Jorge Serrano Elías of Guatemala, Carlos Andrés Pérez of Venezuela, and a long list of other deposed presidents and officials to be named in the final chapter of this volume. The struggle over government accountability is not finished, but the citizen support of El (or La) Que Manda is greatly diminished.

NOTES

1. Nadine Gordimer, "Reflections by Nobel Laureates," in Danieli, Yael, et al., eds., *The Universal Declaration of Human Rights* (Amityville, N.Y.: Baywood, 1999), p. vii.

2. José Lindgren Alves, "The Declaration of Human Rights in Postmodernity," *Human Rights Quarterly* 22, 2 (2000): 478.

3. Paolo G. Carozzo, "From Conquest to Constitutions: Retrieving a Latin American Tradition of the Idea of Human Rights," *Human Rights Quarterly* 25, 2 (2003): 281–313; Mary Ann Glendon, "The Forgotten Crucible: The Latin American Influence on the Universal Human Rights Idea," *Harvard Human Rights Journal* 16 (2003): 27–39. See also her work on the larger process of the creation of the Declaration: *A World Made New: Eleanor Roosevelt and the Universal Declaration of Human Rights* (New York: Random House, 2001).

4. Johannes Morsink, *The Universal Declaration of Human Rights: Origins, Drafting, and Intent* (Philadelphia, PA: University of Pennsylvania Press, 2000).

5. While the contribution of Latin America was noteworthy, Susan Waltz notes historically neglected contributions of other countries in her "Universalizing Human Rights: The Role of Small States in the Construction of the Universal Declaration of Human States," *Human Rights Quarterly* 23, 1 (2001): 44–72.

6. Panama had prior assistance from the American Law Institute.

7. Whether social and economic rights are really rights has been hotly debated. See for example James W. Nickel, "Economic and Social Rights after Fifty Years," *American Philosophical Newsletters* 97, 2 (Spring, 1998): 11–15.

8. For an appreciation of Santa Cruz, see *Hernán Santa Cruz Barceló: Un homenaje en la Cepal* (Santiago: Instituto de Estudios Internacionales de la Universidad de Chile, 2000).

9. Brian Tierney argues in his intellectual history that Las Casas's persuasive use of the language of natural rights was a systematic grafting of the juridical language of Roman and canon law onto Aquinas's views of natural law. See Tierney's *The Idea of Natural Rights: Studies on Natural Rights, Natural Law and Church Law, 1150–1625* (Atlanta: Scholars Press, 1997): 255, 272–87.

10. Gustavo Gutiérrez, *Las Casas: In Search of the Poor of Jesus Christ* (Maryknoll, NY: Orbis Books, 1993).

11. Lascasian studies is a well-established field that benefited from recent historical research by Helen Rand Parish, Lewis Hanke, Isacio Pérez Fernández, and others. For further information on Las Casas, see website maintained by the author of this volume and by historian Lawrence Clayton: lascasas.org.

12. *La Controverse de Valladolid* was directed as a televised film by Jean-Daniel Verhaeghe.

13. For analysis of the debates, see, for example: Lewis Hanke, *All mankind is one; a study of the disputation between Bartolomé de Las Casas and Juan Ginés de Sepúlveda in 1550 on the intellectual and religious capacity of the American Indians* (DeKalb, IL: Northern Illinois University Press, 1974).

14. Paolo G. Carozza expands on this idea in his "They Are Our Brothers and Christ Gave His Life for Them: The Catholic Tradition and the Idea of Human Rights in Latin America," *Logos* 6, 4 (2003): 81–103.

15. The legend that Las Casas introduced slavery to Latin America was disproved by Isacio Pérez Fernández in his *Bartolomé de Las Casas: Contra los negros?* (México City: Ediciones Esquila, 1991). Pérez argued further that Las Casas was among the first to denounce slavery. See also Alfonso Cerdán Esponera's and others' comments on Las Casas and slavery in various numbers of the journal *Studium* esp. those of 2003.

16. Stephen Judd, "The Indigenous Theology Movement in Latin America: Encounters of Memory, Resistance, and Hope at the Crossroads," in Cleary and Steigenga, *Resurgent Voices*: 210–30; Edward L. Cleary, "Birth of Latin American Indigenous Theology," in Guillermo Cook, ed., *Crosscurrents in Indigenous Spirituality* (New York: Brill, 1997): 171–88.

17. Jose Comblin, *El poder militar* (Salamanca, Spain: Sigueme, 1978), 211.

18. Simón Bolívar, "Jamaica Letter," Sept. 6, 1815.

19. José Martí, *Nuestra América*, many editions.

20. Benjamin Keen, *Latin American Civilization: History and Society, 1492 to Present* and Lewis Hanke, *History of Latin American Civilization: Sources and Interpretations* (both, various editions).

21. Lewis Hanke wrote for readers in Spain and Latin America as well as the United States and published numerous works on Las Casas in both English and Spanish. Benjamin Keen,

after suffering isolation during the McCarthy era, became a major force in Latin American history at Northern Illinois University where he published *Bartolomé de Las Casas in History: Toward an Understanding of the Man and His Work* (1971) and *Essays in the Intellectual History of Latin America* (Boulder, CO: Westview Press, 1998).

22. Christine Kovic, *Mayan Voices for Human Rights: Displaced Catholics in Highland Chiapas* (Austin, TX: University of Texas Press, 2005): 54.

23. Among many accounts of grassroots mobilization in Chiapas, including references to Las Casas, see especially June Nash, *Mayan Visions: The Quest for Autonomy in an Age of Globalization* (New York: Routledge, 2001): 164 and passim. Among works on Ruiz, see Jean Meyer, *Samuel Ruiz en San Cristóbal, 1960–2000* (Mexico City: Tusquets, 2000).

24. Samuel Ruiz García, *En busca de la verdad* (San Cristóbal de Las Casas, Mexico: Editorial Fray Bartolomé de Las Casas, 1999): 17–18.

25. Nash's *Mayan Visions* (ref. above) is a reflection of decades of work in Chiapas and other indigenous regions.

26. M. A. thesis, University of Houston-Clear Lake, 2005.

27. Carozzo, "From Conquest": 313.

28. Mary Ann Glendon, *Rights Talk: The Impoverishment of Political Discourse* (New York: The Free Press, 1991).

29. Edward L. Cleary and Timothy J. Steigenga, "Resurgent Voices, Politics, and Religion in Latin America," in Cleary and Steigenga, eds., *Resurgent Voices in Latin America: Indigenous Peoples, Political Mobilization, and Religious Change* (New Brunswick, NJ: Rutgers University Press, 2004): 1–24.

30. Alves: 478–500.

31. Enrique Peruzzotti, "Demanding Accountable Government: Citizens, Politicians, and Governability in Contemporary Argentina," in Steven Levitsky and María Victoria Murillo, eds., *Argentine Democracy* (University Park, PA: Pennsylvania State University, 2005): 233.

2

Women and Rights in Latin America

Latin American women have gained more rights and better treatment than women in the rest of the world.

—New York Times (June 13, 1999)

When Emma Berrazueta de Madrid became one of the first women to graduate from high school in Ecuador in 1939, she had to attend a boys school. There were no academic secondary schools for girls, despite Ecuador being the first Latin American country to allow women to vote in 1929. Señora Berrazueta, now a great grandmother, can look with contentment on the situation of her female descendants and on a much-improved situation for women in Latin America.

These gains impress editorial writers of the *Times* and many other observers. We shall trace here the achievements, but women in Latin America are far from being fully satisfied by the political and legal status they enjoy. More profoundly, women continue to bear double and triple burdens economically and socially. Latin America's increased involvement in a globalized economy has brought greater levels of poverty that especially affect women. We shall examine these, as well.

The following sections take up what is largely new to Latin America. The offenses committed against women and men under military regimes were a major part of Latin American history of the late twentieth century but, in many unusual ways, the crimes brought on response and empowerment. Women arose to become a major force in the human rights response that took place. Second, after military rule, the emphasis on human rights spread to a wide variety of women's rights. Women found new space in society to call wide attention to the economic burden they bore and to the evils of a sexist society in which machismo should no longer be taken for granted. Third, a discernible women's movement has begun and offers contrast to the United States. Fourth, a major marker for women's advancement has been the growing participation of women in politics. Lastly, the so-called morality issues, as of abortion and same-sex civil unions, are taken up.

ORDEAL AND CHANGE

In the remarkable measure that women have made progress in Latin America, part of the explanation lies in the period (1964–1990) when much of Latin America fell under military rule. Women came from traditional roles played at home or as market sellers to become the majority of members in the human rights groups. These organizations formed part of the great human rights movement that opposed military and state repression where these existed.[1] For the first years of the human rights movement women did not typically occupy the top leadership positions. Later, they increasingly became the main leaders of human rights groups and movements.

Women also suffered extensively from state-sponsored terrorism in the period that roughly ran from 1964 to 1990. Some women were killed; many were tortured and raped. However, since the vast majority of those killed or disappeared (and subsequently believed to be dead) were men, women for some time received less attention. The female relatives of the killed or disappeared lived on in greater poverty and often in shame because of some putative crime committed by husband or male relative. Judith Zur demonstrated vividly the loss of status, income, and dignity by Guatemalan Indian women.[2] This history could be recounted in many other countries. Much more than victimhood occurred. Gender relations began shifting. In Guatemala members of CONAVIGUA, a largely women's group, found the courage to criticize the military regime for what Sarah Ratcliffe calls "a gendered violence."[3] One should add, as well: gendered response. Clearly, analysts can no longer ignore the changes in gender relations that are a crucial component of Latin American society.[4]

The recognition of the damage invoked upon women and men in Latin America continued into the twenty-first century, promoted primarily by women. Perhaps the most recognizable logo for Latin American human rights has become the white scarf of the Argentine Mothers of the Plaza de Mayo.[5] When Norberto Kirchner became president of Argentina he said: "We are all Mothers of the Plaza de Mayo." The symbol of their doggedness and courage spans thirty years of activity. The Madres of the Plaza de Mayo continue to march every Thursday afternoon in front of Argentina's presidential palace. Their tenacity is matched in few other places in the world.

More is involved in the long-suffering presence of the Mothers of the Plaza (now often grandmothers) than personal hurt or the demand for the accounting of what happened to an imprisoned relative or a kidnapped grandson or granddaughter. The Madres keep alive a presumed societal need for accounting about the individual and institutional authors of the crimes. (Note the contrast: Spanish and Portuguese women never mounted a similar protest about gross human rights violations in Franco's Spain or Salazar's Portugal.)

One of the innovations of late twentieth century was women telling their story in a public way. They did this in best sellers, as those of Isabel Allende's *Of Love and Shadows*, but more commonly they did so in small but public ways. In Chile, women affected by the killings and disappearances found little help from the government, which continued to deny knowledge of the disappearances. Instead, many women were often sheltered by the Catholic Church. In Santiago they came together on church premises. Guided by therapists, they met in groups and proceeded to tell one another the critical events of their life. From these oral histories they also made crudely fashioned but deeply poignant wall hangings. The government forbade sale of these *arpilleras*, so missionary priests and sisters smuggled them out to the United States, Canada, and Europe. Their stories were thus broadcast to transnational audiences. These weavers also were publicized in concerts by Sting, in documentary movies, as *A Dance of Hope*, and books by Marjorie Agosín, especially her *Tapestries of Hope*.[6]

Women in Peru also produced the colorful wall hangings to tell their stories. Further Peruvian women led the way toward creating theatrical productions of what occurred. Traveling theatrical companies in Peru, Guatemala, and elsewhere moved from village to village to mount dramatic narrations in village squares. They reinforced their message by accepting hospitality from villagers, continuing conversations related to the dramas depicted. These groups tended to play to lower-class Indian and mestizo communities. Among middle-class production companies, probably the best known were the Chilean women who moved from place to place, dancing without partners and with pictures of missing relatives. In 1989, they became the centerpiece of the first victory celebration in the national stadium during the beginning of the end of the Pinochet regime.[7]

AFTER MILITARY RULE

The period after military or authoritarian (in the case of Mexico) rule was intense and creative for women in society. They ascended to government posts, led the way in dealing with the abuses of the past, called attention to the sexism of their societies, began to combat domestic violence, contested *la postestad marital*, and made relatively great gains in being elected to national legislatures.

When the military left presidential palaces, successor governments typically formed governmental agencies to educate civil society in the rights demanded by newly developing democracies. Countries positioned these new human rights agencies within differing government structures. Argentina created a subsecretariat for human rights with the Ministry of Government and Justice. In addition, most countries followed the European lead and created ombudsmen to deal with human rights complaints against the government. Since women had assumed leadership in nongovernmental human rights organizations, it became an easy step for them to move into governmental positions.

However, the acceptance of governmental employment was criticized by many human rights activists for the quieting of the protest impulse and the co-optation of private initiative. Nonetheless, major figures in NGOs took up key posts in government agencies, often for a limited time to attempt to make a contribution before turning to work in NGOs, private law practice, or university teaching.

Memory, Justice, and Reconciliation

Societies have been oppressed by governments for centuries. State-sponsored terrorism has been practiced to an equal or greater degree than Latin America during periods in Europe, Asia, and Africa. Almost never, with the exception of the Nuremberg trials, have these societies attempted either establishing a historical record of what was done or holding government leaders accountable for the injustices. Not true in Latin America where that region cut a pioneering path in demanding accountability for the past. Women have been in the forefront of demanding that some public historical record be written and some authorities brought to trial.

Their inquietude never seems to let up. All countries, with the exception of Uruguay, have created a public record of state terrorism. The records of human rights violations created and the accountability for the crimes acknowledged in various countries were imperfect but considered to be sufficient for nations to move forward. A consensus formed among political and many civic leaders to move on after these accountings to construct democratic institutions after authoritarian rule.

The consensus for shutting the door on the past has not held. Human rights advocates, especially among women survivors, have demanded more accounting for what happened. Despite what seemed to North Atlantic observers to be exemplary memory commissions, Chile, Argentina, Mexico, and Brazil have been convulsed by new demands to examine the past. To take one example, Chile's Rettig Commission conducted a thorough, clean, and transparent investigation of death and disappearance committed mostly by military and police forces in the country. The report was widely publicized and reparations paid. On the surface, national closure on the past occurred.

The ghosts of the past were far from being laid to rest. Small, seemingly unimportant, sectors of Chilean society continued to press demands for a fuller and more satisfactory (to them) accounting. Two groups were especially influential. Relatives of the 2,000–3,000 disappeared wanted to know what happened to their relatives and to have their bodies properly buried. The military, which kept excellent records, should know. Their demands were mediated by the Catholic Church that sponsored a Mesa de Diálogo (Dialogue Roundtable) with representatives of the military. Another group, Chileans Against Torture, would not let die the issue of torture that had been conducted systematically by the military and police at some periods of military rule. This group was mostly noisy but without mainline political or civic support. Among the four major human rights sectors in Chile the antitorture sector was the most marginal. From 1992 these groups pressed on persistently until Christian Democrat governments gave in and created the Valech Commission. One could rightly judge the effort to obtain this monumental step was especially due to women's participation.

In 2004, as the Valech Commission delivered its three-volume report to the president, the nation was transfixed. Some 27,000 persons had been tortured. They would receive lifetime pensions of about $200 a month. Much more was achieved. Chileans had a fuller and undeniable view of what had taken place to ordinary people. Pro-Pinochet sectors had been about 45 percent of the population in 1990, and the whole Chilean society could see the extent of the national wound. In the author's view, women had their way. They had the right to go on living honorably.

Chile was not only fortunate to have impetus from the grassroots for this effort. By the early part of the millennium a woman was defense minister. She contributed to the admission of the army that as *an institution* (not merely as isolated individuals) it had tortured and committed other human rights violations. The army chief of staff apologized publicly.

Michelle Bachelet, the defense minister, is as emblematic of change for women as Emma Berrazueta, mentioned at the top. Bachelet is the daughter of an army general who served under Socialist (and Marxist) Salvador Allende. After her father was killed in interrogation by General Pinochet's army, Bachelet was taken by her mother to Australia and Europe. Bachelet became a pediatric doctor practicing in Chile but, with the democratic opening of politics in 1989–1990, found her interests shifting to the public order. As Chile created civilian control of the military, Bachelet was sent to a university in the United States in preparation for joining the defense ministry where she quickly became the minister. Her performance was exemplary in most regards and Bachelet became president of Chile in 2006.

From Human Rights to Women's Rights

The transition from military to civilian rule brought a great expansion of human rights, previously defined in terms of death, disappearance, and torture, to concern for other rights. From concentration on stopping government killing, torture, and unjust imprisonment, women began to claim a far wider range of rights. This transition began before the military left government as women gathered without publicity to discuss rights and to make tentative plans to widen the definition of rights. With the new freedom of democracy, the creative visions of what societies should look like took more definite and realistic shape. Women demanded freedom from sexual harassment, equality in the workplace, and other rights. They found the public voice they did not have.

The justice of their demands also found a hearing, limited though it was from political parties and democratizing governments. Since many national and regional human rights groups acquired transnational partners during the dictatorships or during the long authoritarian rule of one party in Mexico, Latin American women found in their international partners ready mentors for a much wider struggle for rights.

When the *New York Times* writer could claim Latin American women have made greater progress than other regions, she could have pointed out that all Latin American countries created a cabinet post for women. Further, governments organized agencies within their governments to promote women's interests. These were created in the period from 1981 to 1990. These departments or agencies have persons charged with addressing the many structural problems, such as employment and pay, cultural problems, and harassment associated with *machismo*. The agencies range from Peru's Ministry for the Promotion of Women and Human Development to Honduras's National Institute for Women.

Machismo and Domestic Violence

When interviewed in Quito, Rosario Utreras, a regional director within the Consejo Nacional de la Mujer explained that, while she and her associates at the agency worked at producing educational materials to combat sexist behavior, she put most of her own energies toward providing safe houses where abused women could escape from dangerous situations. She pointed with pride to one facility that offered shelter and assistance to 3,000 women a year. Utreras also focused on increasing women's police stations or services to women after rape or spousal abuse. Lastly, reflecting her own educational and professional experience she worked closely with high schools and universities to open up educational opportunities that led to occupations for women beyond teaching and social work. Yes, she kept Emma Berrazueta de Madrid in mind while doing this.

Utreras's and many others' efforts to reduce domestic violence have pushed this as a priority for the last twenty years in Latin America. The evolutionary progress that has taken place can best be summarized as changing domestic violence from being a private issue into a serious policy concern. Public attention has been called to the prevalence of the problem. Almost half of Latin American women reported psychological abuse, while one to two women in five experience physical violence.[8] With those kinds of percentages in hand, Caroline Moser and Cathy McIlane have argued that the family is a primary site of social violence.[9]

Violence against women remains widespread, especially in the less developed countries such as Honduras. The Penal Code of the country classifies domestic violence and sexual harassment as crimes, with penalties of two to four years and one to three years imprisonment, respectively. Despite these penalties, the Pan-American Health Organization reported that 60 percent of Honduran women had been victims of domestic violence, while the United Nations Population Fund estimated that eight of every ten women suffered from domestic violence. During 2003 only 3,430 cases of domestic violence and 275 cases of rape were reported to police and many fewer cases tried.[10]

Honduran laws against domestic violence lacked some effective deterrents since the laws imposed no fines and only twenty-four-hour preventative detention could be imposed. Honduras created a Special Prosecutor for Women in the Public Ministry. The office was busy, receiving daily about thirty complaints about domestic violence. Beginning in 2002, the government made progress toward resolving more cases through funding special courts to hear only cases of domestic violence.

The incremental progress made in Honduras owes much to women, especially the very poor who are organizing. "Domestic violence" in Honduras used to refer to state-sponsored violence against government-opposition organizations, especially leftist ones. Central America was convulsed by revolution and counterrevolution, especially in the 1980s. Honduras was drawn into the conflict and its military targeted not only leftists but human rights groups that organized to protest death, disappearance, and torture in Honduras without due process. Women's groups existed before this period but two peasant groups, the Honduran Federation of Peasant Women and the Council of Integral Development of Peasant Women, expanded greatly in the 1980s to include some 400 groups, many of them representing the poorest.

From protesting state violence, the emphasis in Honduras began to shift to violence and discrimination against women. By the time peace gained control in the region (1992–1996), Honduran women had created a Honduran Center for Women's Studies and the Honduran Federation of Women's Associations. The first conducted research on the status of women. The latter group, representing some twenty-five women's groups, provided legal assistance for women and lobbied the government on women's issues.

In many countries, improved government services have been provided for women, men, and children affected by the violence. However, the role of the media in reducing domestic violence and advancing other women's issues has been underutilized or, worse, fostered violence in households. A study by Colombia's National Television Commission found that popular *telenovelas* (day and night soap operas) averaged 315 violent scenes a day.[11]

In sum, dramatic changes occurred worldwide in the 1990s, including the ways in which countries treat domestic violence issues. A large number of states no longer treat this violence as a private but rather a public affair and accept some responsibility in preventing violence in the home and in prosecuting offenders. "Nowhere is this change in state discourse and practices more evident than the Americas," state Darren Hawkins and Melissa Humes.[12] Some Latin American countries were among the first in the world to address domestic violence issues and to make this kind of violence a crime.

Recognition of the Economic Burdens of Women: Poverty, Race, and Class

In contrast to the Panglossian belief that the world gets better, Latin America's socioeconomic recession in the 1980s brought a downward trend. Even in 1992 per capita product was still 7 percent lower than in 1980, with greater percentages of Latin

Americans slipping into poverty levels. Many Latin Americanists, to their credit, were quick to call attention to the feminization of poverty that took place in that decade and thereafter. The income levels of families with women heads-of-household (without the presence of a male spouse) deteriorated even faster than the general downward trend in income.

For Afro or Indian women racial discrimination further affected them and their families even more than other social sectors. Anthropologists, tracking these women in cities and in rural areas (where no statistical data gatherers went), called this a triple burden and further noted the courage with which the burdens were carried.

Lack of marital status often compounded economic burdens for women. Less than half of men and women are legally married in a majority of Latin American countries.[13] Consensual unions often last for decades, are frequently associated with profound poverty, and leave women and children bereft of legal claims against spouses and remedies for injustices. Further, when driven by machismo, men frequently act violently against female partners, are financially irresponsible, and have a number of sexual partners.

The number of single women heading urban households is about one in four. The vast majority of these women are responsible for their nuclear family members. The percentage of single women as heads of households grew from 21 to 23 percent in the period 1980–1990. These households grew due to aging of the population, women's greater longevity, and their growing propensity to avoid both marriage and consensual unions. Countries vary greatly in the occurrence of women heading households, from 36 percent in Nicaragua to Mexico with 18 percent.

Recognition of Machismo and a Sexist Society

While machismo is presumed to influence behavior in Latin America and, for that matter, in Mediterranean Europe and Africa, few studies have been conducted to show its prevalence or influence on behavior.[14] Further, a counterculture exists among many of the forty million Indians of Latin America whose views of gender relations differ from those presumed to be present in dominant cultures. One of the few transnational studies of cultural barriers to the improvement of women's status in society has been conducted by Pippa Norris and Ronald Inglehart. They researched obstacles that hold back or facilitate women's participation in politics worldwide.[15] They showed that culture matters: egalitarian attitudes towards women in office are more widespread in postindustrial societies and facilitate their holding political office. They conclude that extensive educational and public-awareness campaigns may have an effect on improving women's status. However, they see educational campaigns as short-term measures and machismo as embedded and only slowly changing.

Latin American women and men promoting change are not waiting for these long-term effects to take place. They have attempted an array of measures, including a high number of legislative proposals. For example, in Chile, in the period from 1990 to 1997, twenty-four legislative proposals on women's rights were introduced. The state agency for women, SERNAM, was important in this process. Anna Liesl Haas also showed that these opportunities for Chilean women to influence legislation increased an independent role for congress and for feminist organizations to influence congress, in relation to a dominant executive role.[16]

Major Gains in Education and Health

Among legislative goals for the advancement of women, parity with men in education has been a major target. The World Bank noted major gains in Latin America, stating that girls and young women have overtaken boys and young men in educational attainment.[17] Latin American data show more girls than boys in both grade and high school enrollment in nearly all the countries of the region, on par with developed countries. In higher education, Latin American women exceeded young men in enrollment at that level in eight countries and were close to the norms of developed countries, but far ahead of other developing areas of the world. One should note that greater progress has been made in terms of achieving equity between men and women in education than other areas of social differentiation in Latin America. However, education is a pivotal factor leading to improved occupational and income opportunities and prestige.

For the poorest and most ignored, some outstanding advances have been made in unlikely places. The second poorest country in the region, Bolivia, ranked first in the world in 2005 for progress it made toward parity for girls in education. For a variety of reasons, such as discrimination against women and lack of separate bathroom facilities, parents in poor countries held girls out of schools. For most of its history, Bolivian women were notably behind men in school enrollment until educational reforms were undertaken in the 1980s. By 1990, only ten percent of girls were less likely to attend primary school. By 2005, girls were as numerous as boys in grade school. The last spurt was attributed to the 1995 Education Reform Law. Other Latin American countries— Mexico, Cuba, and Costa Rica—also made notable gains for women in education.

The health sector reflects great diversity in women's health among nations. Chile's maternal mortality rate rests at sixty-five per 100,000, while Colombia is 100 and Haiti is 600. Overall, women have made notable gains for their own and their family's health. Some of these gains are reflected in the Mothers Index (see Table 2.1). This index includes a number of measures for women's and children's well-being. By 2005, most Latin American countries moved to impressive positions on the world rankings. All but Guatemala and Haiti were in the top half.

Nonetheless, lower-class women and families throughout the region continue to be at much higher risk of illness and death than higher-class women. What is new and encouraging is that well-designed and well-implemented efforts to reform the health systems of the region are underway in some countries through efforts of community

Table 2.1. Mothers Index, 2005

Country	Ranking
Costa Rica	12
Cuba	13
Argentina	17
Chile	17
Mexico	20
Colombia	22
Panama	22
Uruguay	23 (on Children's Index)
Venezuela	31
Dominican Republic	33
Ecuador	38
Nicaragua	40
El Salvador	45
Honduras	45
Paraguay	47
Peru	47
Brazil	50
Bolivia	53
Guatemala	72
Haiti	85

Source: Save the Children Organization, 2005. Data were gathered for six indicators of women's status and four indicators of children's status. (The United States was ranked 10th.)

leaders and women's advocates. They have been able to create public awareness for critical gender-specific dimensions of the supply of and the demand for health services.

Women's Movements

Not only had many women gained experience as the majority of participants in human rights activism, they formed the largest number of persons who participated in the wider universe of new social movements in Latin America. Social movements in the megapolis of São Paulo had 80 percent women participants.[18] This was typical of many cities. In some rural areas mass movements, such as that of the Landless, also drew a majority of female members. Many of these movements focused on survival and provision of public services. The social movement experience transformed gender consciousness. At a minimum, women in survival movements began to reject violence against themselves and to insist on their right to leave the household to participate in neighborhood or citywide groups. This experience also gave women the hope that they could advance their own interests in an exclusionary society and the skills to do so.

A major symbol that came from social movements at the grassroots, in the *favelas* (slums), was Benedicta da Silva. She appears in a video filmed for the Annenberg series, *Americas*, that millions of university students have viewed. At the time of the filming in the early 1990s, Benedicta was one among many *favela* dwellers who became known for their local or regional activism and involvement in party politics. Since the filming she became the first Afro-Brazilian-elected state governor and a prominent face in Brazilian national politics.[19]

In sum, women engaged in politics affected daily life, and they modified it. In the process women created autonomous organizations, increasingly pulling away from male *patrones*, be they union, church, or political leaders. They heard their own voices and they gained a measure of independence. For some women this was a heady experience that propelled them to a combativeness that was focused on gaining their own rights and political offices.

Ethnology of Change

Observers of change among Latin American women can point to women active in society in ways that were not common thirty years ago, but the processes by which the change came about have been largely hidden from view of political scientists and journalists. By contrast, ethnologists observing everyday life over four decades have much to say, although political scientists may be tempted to dismiss as trivial the description of the small steps by which women have gained a measure of empowerment.

One of the most studied sectors is a number of Latin American women—perhaps several million—who became active either in Christian Base Communities (commonly designated CEBs) or in Pentecostal churches.[20] Participation in these groups led women to treat men in incrementally new ways at home and in public life. Moving into new spheres of social relations changed women's views of themselves and, little by little, changed their patterns of interaction with male partners at home or male associates in civic, religious, or political organizations. Within CEBs or Pentecostal groups, women were expected to read Scripture, to interpret its meaning publicly, and to deal with a much more expanded set of social relations than the family. These communities and similar ones within secular, even Marxist, organizations gave women experiences that made easier the building-up of civil society that has occurred through movement activity.

From their households and local church communities women moved farther afield to attend citywide meetings or to travel to state or national capitals. These transhousehold and translocal experiences were the springboard for propelling women into politics. Increasingly, one could note, as the author has done, women ignoring the subtle signs given by men that men are not to be interrupted by women while speaking and that men ultimately decide. In a word, many Latin American women acted as if equality with men was the norm in the rough-and-tumble world of public life.

They believed equality with men was their birthright after absorbing the messages of various ideologies, including liberation theology, Pentecostal independence of conscience, or socialist equality. Women read the scriptural or socialist messages for themselves, had to interpret what the messages meant for them and their families, and were supposed to do something about the messages. In a Catholic small community's methodology, this meant: see-judge-act. All were steps toward independence. Similar methodologies exist in other Christian religions. Such methodologies may also exist in Cuban and Chilean socialism but the argument need not be made here.

Women in Christian communities have further advantages. As John Burdick points out, many church organizational matters are a special province of female expertise:[21] raffles and church fairs, home visits, church adornment, and after-church instruction. When lay participation became the cornerstone of Vatican II reform in Latin America, women began to speak with authority about things they knew best within the church and moved on to increasingly contest men incrementally in other areas. Women had more flexible schedules and numerical preponderance within church groups to challenge men in the organizations.

Opportunities Seized or Lost

The opening to democracy offered a space for discussion of major issues in society. This opening provided women with an opportunity to put forth their views of women in society and their demands for change. This period of *abertura* (openness) was not long. Opportunities to make new claims for women had to be perceived and to be acted on in a matter of months before the structural and constitutional bases of the new democracies were set. Women in the two largest countries, Brazil and Mexico, notably used or lost valuable openings to change.

One could bet the Brazilian women would be the most effective, based on their previous track record of constitutional advances for children and other notable achievements. Both Brazil and Mexico had been under authoritarian rule. In the transition to democracy in both countries, women had new political spaces open for them. Brazilian women, too, had the lead in helping to set up special police stations and for calling attention to domestic violence as a major social issue. However, their attempt to pass effective domestic violence legislation stalled in the early 1990s.

In contrast, Mexican women who had been under the dominance of one-party rule moved quickly and effectively. When authentically competitive legislative elections were held in 1997 for the first time since 1929, women extracted support from eight political parties to support legislation on women's issues. Parties submitted legislation on domestic violence in November 1997 and had legislation approved one month later. Darren Hawkins and Melissa Humes conclude: "Women groups acting autonomously set the agenda for Mexico's political parties rather than vice versa, a rare occurrence in the history of Mexican politics."[22]

Difference or Equality?

Given the new emphasis on the rule of law as the foundation of democracy, women had as a primary goal changing constitutions and national laws to recognize some version of equality or special status of women. These effects reflected basic discussions among women and their allies about whether the discourse about the public role for women should be framed in terms of no essential difference in men and women or in terms of the special, say, maternal or relational, role of women. Both difference and equality have been put forward by women theorists as rationales for better treatment of women in public life in Latin America.

To some extent the difference argument has worked better in Latin America. Men and women, caught in traditional culture, presume differences, even though many aspects of the argument are unproven: assuming maternal and nurturing roles gives women a unique perspective that should be incorporated into political life. Women, it was argued, should not be restricted to private domains. In this perspective, women may be superior to men in their presumptive instinct to care for others and to place the interests of family, group, and nation before their own interests. This kind of talent would thereby improve the conduct of politics. It might even lead to the abolition of militarism and war.

Rosiska Darcy de Oliveira, director of Brazil's National Council of Women's Rights with a doctorate from the University of Geneva, has written along these lines. Her *In Praise of Difference: The Emergence of Global Feminism* has received wide circulation through academic circles. Mary Dietz quickly disputed this claim in her "Context Is All," as others also responded negatively.[23] Nonetheless, many Latin Americans have placed high valorization of women's mothering role, sometimes characterized as "Marianism" (imitating Mary, the Mother of Jesus). Indeed, Mothers of the Plaza de Mayo are an abiding symbol for the search for human rights in Latin America because of being mothers and grandmothers. Nothing like it exists in terms of fathers.

Many women prefer to argue for equality for all human beings: equal opportunity to compete for educational opportunity (especially university professional education) and occupational position, equal pay for equivalent work, and equal consideration for political office. They have made considerable progress. Some Mexican universities routinely pay men and women equally in ways that universities in the United States do not.[24]

A number of Latin American feminists believe that both approaches can used in practice. Elizabeth Jay Friedman examined the creation of the Venezuelan Labor Code to show how women achieved the right to work on equal terms with men (a major symbolic victory). Pregnant and nursing women also were granted special provisions and protections. She noted that protections were granted not to all women but to those women who are mothers and that motherhood was a function for society generally and not a private issue.[25] Tensions between the two approaches will probably never be resolved. However, Latin American women, in the author's view, cooperate to work out their differences and to form coalitions better than many feminist theorists or activists in North Atlantic countries.

Women have faced many walls of cultural and legal constraints. In the extreme cases, Argentine and Chilean military governments emphasized *la potestad marital*, giving men full control over the person and property of their wives. More commonly laws, employment policies, jobs, and pay scales tended to work against parity for women. Political parties had few places on their electoral slates for women and government in the higher reaches of civil service had even fewer places.

In a sense, Latin America's military did women a favor by politicizing the private sphere of the family, moving women to social action, and offering them a stimulus for moving from inertia in the public sphere to opposition to the government.[26] This was especially true in Argentina, the site of the worst military crimes against its people. The women's movement arose from several bases of mobilizations, especially from women providing survival resources for their families and from women relatives of the thousands of disappeared. The Argentine women's movement, working with the democratizing governments, accomplished these goals: modified *la potestad marital*, legalized divorce, extended child care facilities, made contraceptive devices available, and caused a wide discussion of domestic violence.

These achievements and others like them were accomplished in the early stages of democratization. Since then, feminist scholars have noted with regret the slow progress of women's issues in Latin American politics and society. The time of opportunity when redefinition of gender roles and machismo practices were up for grabs has largely passed, and Latin Americans have reverted, to some degree, to their cultural propensity for machismo. This trend to return to uncontested assertion of power and control over women has been reinforced by the poverty associated with structural adjustments made in the region to globalization and the high unemployment of men that followed. Poverty intensified negative aspects of machismo in violence, financial irresponsibility, and sexual infidelity in families.

Social movements, now better understood after years of historical scholarship, ebb and flow dramatically. On the downslope, after two or three decades of movement activity, participants typically experience a sense of loss and grief. The slow, disappointing progress of women in Chile and Brazil has been traced and analyzed by Carol Drogus and co-authors in a recent work, *Activist Faith*.[27] The women's movement elsewhere has often had a different trajectory. Hence, by contrast to Chile and Brazil, a number of authors have traced the lively world of women organizing and achieving notable success in the edited volume *Women of Chiapas: Making History in Times of Struggle and Hope* and Christine Kovic's *Mayan Voices for Human Rights*.[28]

The women's movement continues in Latin America. In 2001, after more than twenty years' effort, the Brazilian women's movement finally witnessed the Brazilian Congress approve a legal code that made women equal to men in the eyes of the law. The women's movement has become institutionalized, becoming carriers of thirty years' experience, and acts adeptly at choosing targets of opportunity and at protecting constitutional and other legal advances.

WOMEN IN POLITICS

Women presidents in Latin America have numbered fewer than the fingers on one hand. Where gains can best be seen are in cabinet ministers and, even more so, in representation in legislatures. One expects to find a woman or two in presidential cabinets, given the national and international pressures for some women's faces to appear in group photographs. One could further predict that one minister would head the women's governmental agency and another would carry the portfolio for Social Welfare or Health, women's traditional domains. The surprise has been the speed with which Mexico put forward a woman, Rosario Green, as foreign minister, traditionally one of the posts men most crave. Colombia has placed a woman as Minister of Defense, perhaps the most macho post of all. Chile has had women as foreign minister and minister of defense in the same cabinet. Both *chilenas* put themselves forward as presidential candidates in 2006. Michelle Bachelet won the presidency and named ten women and ten men as ministers.

For many analysts the major worldwide indicator of the situation of women in politics has been the percentage of women serving in national legislatures. For a time, women legislators in Latin America hovered at about 10 percent. This has notably improved so that Latin America ranks just below the Nordic nations (Table 2.2). The Americas (here including the United States) stand second in the world, ahead of combined European countries and the other nations of the world.

Twelve Latin American nations exceed the United States in electing women to national legislatures and eight fall behind the United States (Table 2.3). (In the United

Table 2.2. Women in National Legislatures, 2006

Area	Percentages
Nordic countries	40.1
Americas	20.1
Europe, including Nordic	18.4

Source: Information provided on Inter-Parliamentary Union website in February 2006.

Table 2.3. Women in National Parliaments, 2006

Country	Percentages
Argentina	36.2
Cuba	36.0
Costa Rica	35.1
Venezuela	29.9
Honduras	23.4
Mexico	22.6
Nicaragua	20.7
Peru	18.3
Dominican Republic	17.3
Bolivia	16.9
Panama	16.7
Ecuador	16.0
United States	**15.2**
Chile	15.0
Colombia	12.1
Uruguay	11.1
El Salvador	10.7
Paraguay	10.0
Brazil	8.6
Guatemala	8.2
Haiti	3.6
Average Total Percentage	**20.1**

Source: Information provided on Inter-Parliamentary Union website in February 2006.

States, women have fared slightly better in state legislatures with 22.5 percent women in 2005, a percentage held constant for five years.) Argentina, Cuba, and Costa Rica rank in the top ten countries in the world, with 36 to 34 percent of female national legislators.

The velocity with which some Latin American countries increased female representation in national legislatures has been breathtaking, for observers more used to glacial social change for women south of the Rio Grande. Using 1980 or 1990 as a baseline, doubling or tripling percentages seems unbelievable. Dramatic increases continue: Peruvian women legislators jumped from 9.7 to 29.2 percent and Honduran women from 5.5 to 23.4 in the 2004 to 2006 rankings. Nonetheless, some countries that offered the most promise for women lag behind.

Why have Brazilian and Chilean women—who stood at the forefront of social movements to oppose military governments or to promote children and family interests—

not made more gains? Brazil has proven to be extremely disappointing to its friends in the transnational human rights movement, with its extremely low 8.6 percent total of women in both legislative houses. The other disappointment, Chile, has much in common with Argentina in historical contexts, gender cultures, and military-directed state-sponsored terrorism. Yet Chile has two-times fewer women national legislators than Argentina.

To facilitate the entry of women into politics, a number of Latin American countries have adopted quotas: a certain percentage of women have to appear on political party tickets. Researcher Marcela Rios found that, in general, quotas have worked well in Latin America.[29] Indeed, Tricia Gray, writing in 2003, could state that: "Since the 1990s Latin American countries have been in the forefront of the struggle for increased representation and equal rights for women."[30] Twelve Latin American countries passed laws that established a minimum level of 20 to 40 percent for women's participation as candidates in national elections.

Chile and Argentina, side-by-side on so many measures of society and culture, illuminate salient aspects of having quotas or not, and of where to place quotas for the better advance of women in politics. Argentina was the first democratic country (as contrasted to authoritarian Cuba) to adopt a national electoral quota for women in 1991, the *Ley de Cupos*. Argentina skyrocketed to 36 percent of women in the national legislature in less than fifteen years. In contrast, Chile had no *ley de cupos*, and only 15 percent of its legislators are women. Some of its political parties adopted quotas in the 1990s, generally for party leadership and not election tickets. However, the election of Michelle Bachelet as president embolded Chilean women leaders to request 40 percent of the party ballots be women.

Leaders within Chile's advanced democratic system reflected the commonly expressed arguments against electoral quotas. First, competition ought to be based on merit, not quotas. Second, not enough women (as yet) are qualified or willing to fill decision-making roles. Further, Brazil seems to show what happens when arbitrary quota percentages are applied. In the early stage of quotas, Brazilian ballot-makers appeared to be choosing categories before considering specific women and their legislative capabilities, so it was thought proper to look for an Afro and Pentecostal woman to fill out an appropriate place on the ballot. Then, too, some critics have seen quotas as ceilings rather than floors, asking why 30 percent? They view this as a restriction and tokenism.

The InterAmerican Dialogue (IAD) has kept a report card on women in power. Their analysis shows that national quota laws are far more effective than political party quotas. Further, IAD analysts believe that "if quota laws are not tailored to a country's electoral system and applied by electoral parties, they will produce few results for women."[31]

Another comparison of Argentina to its large neighbor, Brazil, bears out the argument that having quotas is not enough. Both countries have quotas but far different results have followed. Brazil's federal law in 1997 mandated the posting of 30 percent women on electoral lists but political parties have not shown the willingness to meet the quota, according to Almira Rodrigues, director of the Center for Feminist Research and Consulting (CFEMEA). She concludes that parties failed to invest in female candidates and to stimulate women's participation.[32] Even in the 2004 municipal council elections (where earliest gains for women entering politics are typically noted), women only won 12.65 percent of the seats.[33] Among Brazil's twenty-seven parties, the percentage of women elected tended to range between 10 to 15 percent, with no party having more than 17 percent success.

SOCIO-SEXUAL ISSUES

To the amazement of a number of scholars, including demographers, "Catholic" Italy had the lowest birth rate in the world; Spain was almost as low. Birth rates have dropped impressively through much of Latin America. This has been a quiet development in contrast to abortion that has received greater attention. Many Latin Americans have argued that more than individual sexual rights are involved in abortion and argue for the protection of life. Nonetheless, considerable change has been made in the last twenty years. Nearly all the countries of the region permit abortion under limited conditions—for preserving the life or health of the mother or under conditions of rape or incest.

Chile stands virtually alone in not allowing abortion for any reason. Tim Fresca, an author resident in Chile, believes the country is an anomaly and that abortion is still too taboo as a public issue to allow serious debate.[34] The most conservative countries, Colombia and Mexico, did enter into resolute debate. Colombia, since 2001, has been moving toward removal of legal penalties for abortion. Its Constitutional Court ruled in 2006 in such a way that allows abortion in cases of rape, fetal abnormalities, and danger to the life of a woman. The Federal District of Mexico City now allows abortion under similar circumstances. While much attention was given the debate over divorce in Chile, divorce in Mexico was much easier to obtain than in the United States during the 1930s. Indeed, Tijuana and other Mexican cities served as refuges for Hollywood stars seeking an relatively easy divorce. Then, fifty years later, the "Dominican quickie" attracted many from the east coast of the United States to the Dominican Republic through ads in the Yellow Pages in the United States. Thus, Chilean prohibition of civil divorce made the country an even greater anomaly until Chile made divorce legal in March 2004.[35]

Lesbian and gay rights proposals and legislative debates about civil union or gay marriage are proceeding at about the same velocity as in the United States. The first Latin American gay couple to have achieved legal recognition occurred in Buenos Aires, July 13, 2003. This legal ceremony was followed in the Southern Brazilian state of Rio Grande do Sul that registered a civil union for a gay couple in March 2004. In

Colombia, when the issue of legalizing homosexual unions was brought to the Senate in August 2003, it was defeated but still received considerable support, 55 to 32. In Chile, a civil-union proposal started its way through Parliament in June 2003. A widening of legislative initiatives, defeats, and successes is expected to follow.

CONCLUSION

Within two decades women in Latin America have moved to parity with Europe in an important measure of women in national legislatures. As a developing area, Latin America has moved much more quickly than Africa and Asia. The obstacles women face are mountainous but no longer seem unconquerable. Moreover, women are helping to spearhead other human rights issues, as will be seen in other chapters of this volume.

NOTES

1. Military governments of the 1960s and 1970s in Ecuador, Panama, and Peru did not leave a legacy of human rights violations, as the Southern Cone countries did.

2. Judith Zur, *Violent Memories: Mayan War Widows in Guatemala* (Boulder, CO: Westview, 1998).

3. Sarah Ratcliffe, "Civil Society, Grassroots Politics, and Livelihoods," in Robert N. Gwynne and Cristóbal Key, eds., *Latin America Transformed* (New York: Oxford University Press, 2nd ed., 2004): 201.

4. See, for example, Diane Nelson's *A Finger in the Wound: Body Politics in Quincentennial Guatemala* (Berkeley: University of California Press, 1999), a work suffused with gender considerations.

5. A somewhat similar group exists in Chile.

6. Marjorie Agosín, *Tapestries of Hope, Threads of Love: The Arpillera Movement in Chile, 1974–1994* (Albuquerque, NM: University of New Mexico Press, 1996).

7. The documentary film *Dance of Hope* commemorates the group but offers no name for the group.

8. Andrew R. Morrison and María Loreto Biehl, eds., "Introduction," *Too Close to Home: Domestic Violence in the Americas* (Washington: Inter-American Development Bank, 1999): xi.

9. Caroline Moser and Cathy McIlwane, *Encounters with Violence in Latin America: Urban Poor Perceptions from Colombia and Guatemala* (New York: Routledge, 2004).

10. US Department of State, Country Reports on Human Rights in Honduras, 2003.

11. Jacquin Strouss de Samper, "The Role of Television in Curbing Violence," in Morrison and Biehl., eds., *Too Close to Home*: 192.

12. Darren Hawkins and Melissa Humes, "Human Rights and Domestic Violence," *Political Science Quarterly* 117, 2 (2002): 131.

13. Teresa Valdes and Enrique Gomariz, eds., *Latin American Women* (Santiago: Facultad Latinoamericana de Ciencias Sociales, 1995): 61.

14. One of the few studies, Matthew C. Guttman's *The Meaning of Being Macho* (Berkeley: University of California Press, 1996), shows the prevalence of male culture in Mexico City, as well as changes in helping with housework and accepting female community leaders.

15. Pippa Norris and Ronald Inglehart, "Cultural Obstacles to Equal Representation," *Journal of Democracy* 12, 3 (2001): 126–40.

16. Anna Liesl Haas, "Legislating Equality: Institutional Politics and the Expansion of Human Rights in Chile," Ph.D. diss., University of North Carolina, Chapel Hill, 2000.

17. News release from World Bank, Oct. 7, 2003, concerning the Bank's 2003 study of inequality.

18. Yvonne Corcoran-Nantes, "Women and Popular Urban Social Movements in São Paulo, Brazil," *Bulletin of Latin American Studies* 9, 2 (1990): xx. See also Joe Foweraker, *Theorizing Social Movements* (Boulder, CO: Pluto Press, 1995): 54.

19. Biography of Benedicta da Silva.

20. Drogus, Hallum, et al.

21. John Burdick, *Legacies of Liberation: The Progressive Catholic Church in Brazil* (Burlington, VT: Ashgate, 2004): 64.

22. Darren Hawkins and Melissa Humes, "Human Rights and Domestic Violence," *Political Science Quarterly* 17, 2 (2001): 255.

23. Mary Dietz, "Context Is All: Feminism and Theories of Citizenship," *Daedalus* 116 (1987): 1–24.

24. Interviews with university professors, National Autonomous University, Mexico City, Nov. 15–23, 1993.

25. Elizabeth Jay Friedman, "Getting Rights for Those without Representation: The Success of Conjunctural Coalition-Building in Venezuela," in Nikki Craske and Maxine Molyneaux, eds., *Gender and the Politics of Rights and Democracy in Latin America* (New York: Palgrave, 2002): 66.

26. Jane Jacquette, "Introduction," in Jacquette, ed., *The Women's Movement in Latin America: Feminism and the Transition to Democracy* (Winchester, MA: Unwin Hyman, 1989): 58.

27. Carol Drogus and Hannah Stewart-Gambino, *Activist Faith: Women from the Popular Church and Social Movements in Democratic Brazil and Chile* (University Park, PA: Pennsylvania State University Press, 2005).

28. Christine Eber and Christine Kovic, eds., *Women in Chiapas* (New York: Routledge, 2003), and Christine Kovic, *Mayan Voices for Human Rights: Displaced Catholics in Highland Chiapas* (Austin: University of Texas Press, 2005).

29. Daniela Estrada, "Latin America: Progress toward Gender Parity in Politics," www.peacewomen.org, viewed June 7, 2007.

30. Tricia Gray, "Electoral Gender Quotas: Lessons from Argentina and Chile," *Bulletin of Latin American Research* 22, 1 (2003): 54.

31. IAD, 2001: 9 (in Tricia Gray, 2003: 55).

32. *Latinamerica Press* 20 (Oct. 6, 2004): 4.

33. CFEMEA-TSE Dados de 08/10/2004.

34. Tim Fresca, "Gaining Ground," *Conscience* (Summer 2003): 23.

35. On Chile see *The Inter-American Dialogue's Latin American Advisor* (March 22, 2004): 1 and 4.

3

Life and Death on the Streets: From Street Children to Children at Risk

When Brazilian policemen opened fire on some sixty street children and killed eight of them, the event opened the eyes of Brazil and people worldwide to a major issue in human rights. The event took place in January 1993 and was called the Candelária Massacre, from the name of the downtown church in Rio de Janeiro alongside of which the massacre took place. No satisfactory judicial conclusion was reached.[1] However, from then on, the issue of street children and adolescents has involved hundred of thousands of persons working at various levels to protect and care for what societies regard as their most vulnerable group, along with the disabled and the elderly.

The issue of street children is closely related to virtually every other issue treated in this volume, especially women's issues and policing and human rights. Further, the issue is tied to what is taking place in globalization, both its negative effects as well as the positive effects of transnational human rights efforts. The problem is worldwide, although homeless children in the United States and developed countries tend to be part of homeless families. The situation seems more acute in Latin America and some other regions where social cleansing is carried out by police or hired gunmen. Mexican and Central American cities and now rural areas have been plagued by youth gang violence. This situation was exacerbated as these illegal immigrants to the United States, where they became adept at violence, returned to their home countries.

The following sections will examine, first, who are "street children." This section will look at the evolving historical views of children and families in Latin America. Then the chapter addresses aspects of human rights as they apply to these children and formation of groups to protect their rights. The final sections take up mobilizing for new laws and decrees and the shift in discourse to children at risk rather than children on the street.

Breaking into Public Consciousness

International travelers have seen an evident change in the urban public spaces of Latin America over the last fifty years. Among the differences are the presences of children sleeping rough after dark, the magnitude of children sniffing glue or using other drugs, and the intimidating quality of begging by young people. There have been children on the streets for centuries. Latin America, except for, say, Uruguay, Costa Rica, and Argentina in this century, never had enough schools for its lower classes. Brazil, even in the early 1990s, lacked classrooms for over four million of its children.

The rapid shift from being mostly rural to being mostly urban changed the character of Latin America's cities and put homeless children on a central stage. When most of a nation's population lived near farms, extended-family living arrangements made sense. When Juan Usipanqui's family moved to Lima in 1975, food became harder to obtain. Juan watched how uprooting from familiar social circles made more difficult the long-standing custom of sharing food. When one household had a windfall of abundance, they shared their food with extended families under nearby roofs. In 1984, Juan lost steady employment and joined millions of unemployed. His family could no longer shelter and feed children of his extended family. Thus, for many, the 1980s brought the final blow to the open family structure. Poor families closed in on themselves for survival. Children appeared increasingly on the streets at night.

Military governments, in power in the 1970s and 1980s, tried to control the problem with force. Military and police enforced nightly curfews and put homeless children and adolescents in detention centers. When the military left governing directly, children and adolescents poured out onto the streets. The last two decades also brought attractive and dangerous wealth to the streets through trade in native-grown coca and marijuana. This commerce demanded structure and networking. So, too, did thievery. Thus, mafia-like families of organized street gangs demanded regular payments from shopkeepers. The groups also marked off their territories for mugging and theft. They patrolled exits of pedestrian tunnels between Rio's beaches and shopping centers. They made the elevators between upper and lower Salvador, Bahía, a risky transit. The most dangerous areas are in Brazil and Colombia. However, nights are unsafe in Central American capitals, as well.

Reactions to crimes by young people, whether the crimes were real or merely suspected, have been swift and lethal. Children and adolescents have been killed by the hundreds each year. An investigation by the Brazilian congress reported 4,611 young persons (most of them Afro-Brazilian) killed between 1990 and 1993.[2] Thousands of others were beaten and tortured.

When Gilberto Dimenstein was putting together his widely read *The War on Children*, he and a photographer visited six of Brazil's largest cities.[3] "It was," he said, "impossible not to be affected by the stories we heard of the torture, ill-treatment, and murder of children. . . . We often spent the day in the sun and many places we visited in the shantytowns stank, but I needed a bath not so much to get rid of the sweat or the smell. It was more a need to wash away all that I had heard; a vague, useless attempt to expunge from my memory words I did not want to hear, like trying to shake the dust from my clothes."[4]

For centuries, extended family or strangers typically cared for children after premature death of parents, even abandonment by parents. Within networks of villages or small urban communities, many Latin American families took in children who were not their own. Women who acted as mothers argued to complaining males that another mouth to feed added little burden.

Orphanages, often run by religious groups, cared for limited numbers of children not living with families. William Wasson's fabled Cuernavaca orphanage encouraged remarkable mutual care among orphans and gained international attention in the 1970s. Even convicted young criminals often found a substitute to jail in low-security alternatives run by groups, such as the Sisters of the Good Shepherd.[5] Such efforts were possible because the scale of the problem was small.

Another kind of orphan began appearing in Latin America's streets. In Europe post-war shoeshine orphans have mostly disappeared. However, in Latin America shoeshine boys, known as *gamines*, increasingly gained attention. Their numbers grew, to the anxiety of religious groups, caring adults, and police. They were a new breed of orphan, independent and older, difficult to deal with. Thus, the category of "street children" has a more recent history and probably can be dated from the time of economic crises in the 1980s, a time in Latin America commonly called the lost decade. During 1980–1992, real wages dropped considerably and many men and women lost their jobs, as Latin American countries dropped their failing state-sponsored capitalist systems and entered the free-market global economy.

Young People in Latin America

Histories of young persons in Latin America are only now being written. They were mostly invisible or were only an appendage to families or adult males who were the makers of history. Yet, enough is known through recent archival research to describe with some confidence what follows. Persons under twenty have been a large portion of the population of the region since colonial times. In the eighteenth century they formed between 30 to 50 percent of the population. As noted in the chapter on women, birthrates dropped dramatically in the twentieth century, but public health campaigns were notably successful and kept alive many young persons who would have perished. The proportion of youth now exceeds 50 percent, giving Latin America the sense of being a young region. Further, the young are a major element in contributing income to families and in draining the budgets of governments attempting to provide education and other services.

The neglect of childhood by Latin American historians derives in part from Spanish and Portuguese views and laws that determined that the care and nurture of children were private functions and fell into the sphere of families. So, historians seldom discussed children of legitimate families. The major obstacle for understanding children and families is cultural: the majority of families are not, nor have they been, nuclear. Nor have most children been born into such families. These statements do not deny that the family was and is the fundamental unit of society.

Hence, the majority of children born in Latin America since 1492 were not born into monogamous marriages. Before the twentieth century, families formed through legal marriages were not the norm, and in the twentieth century, legal marriages continue to be atypical in many countries. Nonetheless, the family, whether consensual or nuclear, is a vital institution. One might view the family better from the point of view of minors. As Elizabeth Kuznesof says, "Children in Latin America utilize kinship and family relations in creative and adaptive ways even as they interact ever more strongly with the globalized economy."[6] In an important sense, children and adolescents run in and out of contact with their families, living in greater or lesser degree on the streets, but with a solid attachment to a family at any one time or perhaps two or more families over time.

Thus, the view of the family imbedded in culture since colonial times was an ideal, something that was thought by many as appropriate for society and morality, but not often attainable. Further, a global model of what family and childhood should be has been promoted.[7] In this vision children should be protected from harsh experiences; they should have time to play and not work full-time; and they should go to school for a fairly long time. This elite vision has never been possible for perhaps the majority of Latin American children. *The Diary of Carolina Maria de Jesus* that thousands of students in Latin American studies have read is much closer to the lived reality of many mothers and children than the lives contained in many Latin American novels.[8]

Kinship, in various forms, including tattered families or what can described as an axis of lives centered on a single mother, is still the most important institution for social stability in the midst of social and economic changes. Kin are counted on both paternal and maternal sides, with kinship recognized even to the seventh or higher degree. Foundations for kinship other than blood are strong in Latin America. The chief basis is *compadraczo/compadrio* (ritual kinship) that brings reciprocal relations. Another basis for familylike bonding was plantation society where extended families included slaves and dependents. These extended families could form a very large group that became interdependent for survival and affective connectivity. Even the willingness to choose one another out of need—intentional families—serves as a substitute for blood relationships. The well-received Brazilian movie *Central Station* exemplified what is happening in contemporary kinship in a globalized world. Older parentlike persons begin to assume responsibility for minors without families, but minors also exercise reciprocal care for adults, as will be emphasized later.

An ethic of protection of children and adolescents evolved in the eighteenth and nineteenth centuries, emphasizing fragility and presumed innocence. Orphanages and benevolent societies protected children that families could not. By custom, even small villages maintained a *casa de mendigos* (beggars' house), a shelter with one room for men and another for women and children, but nineteenth-century legislation already targeted unruly and vagrant youths perceived as a menace to society. Apprenticeships were seen as a useful way to educate young people and keep them out of trouble. When compulsory schooling for persons seven to fourteen was mandated in most Latin American countries in the early twentieth century, vast numbers in the lower classes found no school provided for them. Further, many poor parents were not convinced that schooling would lead their children to good jobs. Again, childhood of the poor was distinct from that of the elite.

The tipping point whereby begging and unruly children on the streets became a "street children" problem accelerated in the last third of the twentieth century. Individuals and families poured into cities, pulled by the prospects of employment and pushed by consolidation of farms or degraded soils, of which there are more than a million hectares in Latin America. In a word, the fundamental reason why there are street children is because there are insufficient resources at home, nowhere to sleep, not enough to eat, no money to pay for necessities.

At the end of the twentieth century, it became clear that poor Latin Americans were creating new alliances and kinship strategies. Street children often provide important resources for the families. Children of the poor are expected from an early age to contribute to the income and welfare of the household. Tobias Hecht claims that many children of the poor have the typical expectations about childhood turned around: they are not nurtured and expected to grow up as consumers; they are nurturing and expected from an early age to contribute. Anyone observing the array of adult cripples begging on the streets of Caracas or Quito will find a ten-year-old pushing the wheelchair or acting in some capacity as agent of the disabled.

Mothers run many Latin American households and are its focal point. As Tobias Hecht writes, "Children see supporting their mothers and nurturing the household as a virtue."[9] He quotes the mother of a dozen children: "My luck in my life is my children, who bring me money and food. . . . I can't work with so many little ones around. Where would I be without them?"[10]

Children leave home gradually as changes take place in that environment. This typically is not sudden. A new stepfather often enters the household or sleeping space becomes problematic. Children are sent out to the streets to bring home resources (money or commodities, begged or stolen). When they remain empty-handed, they fear returning home. Many travel long distances on various modes of crowded public transportation between where they sleep and where they work, growing tired of the long commute. At some point, they begin sleeping in the rough near where they work, often near others their same age. They find another kind of association among other young persons on the streets. Often they alternate for short and long periods between sleeping on the street and at home.

Even while living on the streets most of the time, children respond to questioners that they are working to help their families, traveling to their households to drop off resources.[11] (At least they think they contribute by not taking away sleeping space from others in the household.) The heads of poor households acknowledge their dependency on their children.

STREET CHILDREN AND HUMAN RIGHTS

Virtually all observers are agreed that emphasis on the human rights issues of children, not just street children, has been a powerful step forward. In the process, though, the term street children began to receive diminished usage. Brazil is used here as an extended example because the political and legal issues are exemplified there better than in many other countries. Groups working with street children in Brazil arose under military government (1964–1985).[12] Human rights groups protested against state inaction on street children, against covert state killings or approval of killings, and against the larger socioeconomic system that produced these byproducts.

In Brazil, military control tightened gradually. From a benign *dictablanda* (soft dictatorship) military rulers became increasingly closed to civilian opposition. By 1970 only slight traces of representative politics remained. With authoritarian decrees (especially Institutional Act 5 and succeeding decrees), the military limited oppositional activity of political parties, intellectuals, artists, and the media. Arbitrary detentions, extralegal killings, and torture became systematic. In this context, the Catholic Church was virtually the only institution in society left with public rights. As Ronald M. Schneider says, "The Catholic Church became the chief critic of human rights violations, and to an increasing degree, of social injustice as well."[13] With the protection of the church, human rights groups engaged in protecting persons and groups at risk. Human rights were not well-understood themes in Brazil until military repression tightened in the late 1960s.

The rights of many children had been violated for as long as anyone could remember. The issue became more acute under military rule. When the military took over in 1964, they inherited a repressive system for dealing with abandoned and street children. The notorious Assistance Service to Minors (SAM) conducted correctional facilities. These facilities were intended to be frightening "branches of hell." The press occasionally reported scandals in the decade before the military took over, but little reform occurred.

The first leaders of the military government that lasted twenty-one years tried out an assistance-oriented policy,[14] but the military felt the need to control society more tightly. Thus, the military enacted important new laws that gave the government power to intervene in the lives of minors in "irregular circumstances." As Anthony Dewees and Steven Kless remark, "This policy criminalized the activities of millions of young people, whether they had committed a crime or were simply in the streets seeking to survive."[15]

Military men and other nationalists did not want children on the streets. Order was disturbed by unruly children and adolescents. Further, Brazil's burning desire to become a respected world power fueled a need for a suitable image. Children and adolescents were swept into jails and prisons to get them off the streets. Almost 700,000 children and adolescents would be locked up in State Foundations for the Welfare of Minors (FEBEMs) or related reform schools.[16]

These actions helped mobilize groups in defense of minors. Human rights advocates watched the often callous routines of child welfare institutions such as FEBEMs. Incarceration in Latin America has historically been a grim experience, meant to punish and to terrify, as noted in another chapter.

Movement Commences

Adults working with young street people typically organized themselves into neighborhood groups, took turns being on the street, and offered acceptance and friendship as the first steps toward more extended care in diverse settings. Many adults mobilized as a force through Christian Base Communities (CEBs) and similar neighborhood groups. Some had enough organizational structures to be called NGOs. Their dissatisfactions with the growing problem, the violence of security forces, and callousness of governmental agencies served as the basis for organizing on a wider scale beyond their neighborhoods and cities. Group members who often thought of themselves as nonpolitical found themselves drawn into an increasingly large political arena. They began mounting their discontents as challenges to the system. Their efforts led them into national prominence in ways they would not have dreamed of.

Of all Latin Americans, Brazilians mounted the most prominent human rights movement for children. The environment was not favorable for organizing. Military governors wanted to atomize society, to keep voluntary nongovernmental groups from joining together, and to dictate national policy without opposition. Like their best soccer players, adept Brazilian grassroots groups found subtle ways to express and to channel their deeply felt frustrations over human rights violations. Out of an impulse for charity came a movement for structural change and justice.

Deodato Rivera, with members of the Catholic Justice and Peace Commission, saw for themselves how these conditions affected young prisoners. They found cells contaminated.[17] The rooms had no mattresses, chairs, sheets, or soap. Inmates were forced to sleep on often damp cement floors.

Night was the worst. Weeping and groaning often filled the air. Young persons who had never been in trouble and were not used to being detained gave in to heartbroken feelings in the dark. Other adolescents who had been in jail for months groaned involuntarily, overwhelmed by degrading conditions. Sexual abuse and violence recurred in dreams.

Human rights activists, in increasing numbers, aided children in prison, police centers, and on the streets. They worked at alleviating the worst hardships suffered by the children and adolescents. They provided medical attention, comfort, and aftercare for torture and other abuses.

In working for homeless children's welfare, human rights workers observed that even laws were used as instruments of oppression for Brazilian children. UNICEF noted: "Thousands [of children] were sent off to harsh correctional institutions simply because they were poor and abandoned. Such children had no legal rights, and abuse by police and other authorities had become the norm."[18]

Public Space Opens

Two hundred human rights and activist groups working on behalf of street children had been formed by the time military governments gave way to popularly elected leaders in 1985.[19] Public space opened for the specialized movement for children and adolescent rights. This occurred during the long run-up to civilian rule, known in Brazil as *distensão* (decompression).

Within the military government, first under General Ernesto Geisel and then General João Baptista Figueiredo, some policymakers were searching for alternatives to correctional approaches. Other groups, too, especially the Social Secretariat of the Catholic Church and UNICEF, shared similar convictions about new choices. In the early 1980s, these disparate groups pulled together in a common project, the Alternative Project.

Given the size of Brazil and the atomizing effect of military control on society, organizations working for human rights had been isolated from one another. As the military allowed more political space, groups working with the Alternative Project opened for public debate the correctional model and alternative programs. Working for long months on the Alternative Project brought these groups a common sense of purpose, crucial for social movements.

By November 1984, with the military government winding down, the groups brought the Alternative Project to the final reporting stage. The military's national pride aided the project. Brazil's commanders thought of themselves as the leaders for Latin America and of Brazil as the first nation of the region. Thus, the military government sponsored a meeting on street children for all of Latin America.[20] The media, attuned to reporting what the government fostered, applauded Brazil's leadership and widely publicized the meeting.

The media's interest was key in framing the issue for the movement. Brazilians had referred to street children as *moleques*, as ragamuffins or worse.[21] Now the media portrayed these children in a more favorable light. For the human rights organizers, the timing and the media attention were decisive. The movement for street children was able through the media to gain a collective identity. Through published and televised interviews, members of the sprawling movement talked with one another.

Secondly, movement members projected to the Brazilian public an image of an issue taken seriously by national (including military men in uniforms) and international "authorities." The media attention, then and through the next few years, allowed movement participants to project a strong collective image to opponents. They were trustworthy adults openly critical of government programs. Activists also emphasized children and adolescents as able to speak clearly about the conditions of their lives, the reasons (often survival) they went to the streets, and the nightmarish violence they faced.

Allowing children and adolescents to speak for themselves before national audiences was a master stroke of the movement. Antonio Carlos Gomes da Costa, UNICEF's representative to the Alternative Project, said: "Brazilian society was accustomed to looking at these children exclusively as needy, seeing what they did not have, what they did not know, what they were incapable of, a totally negative profile compared to the middle-class norm. The movement presented street children in a positive light, emphasizing what they could do."[22]

Shaping the Issue

Activist groups participated in government-controlled meetings in which they expressed their opposition to the correctional approach. Within the organizations, members debated how to recast the issue. They decided to shift from emphasizing assistance to rights. In many senses, the movement would succeed or fail based on this objective.

In the process, human rights groups participating in the Alternative Project became a national political movement. They created the National Movement of Street Boys and Street Girls (MNMMR) in 1985. The movement gained premier status around the world. The movement also became first among equals in the Brazilian human rights movement.

MOBILIZING FOR A NEW CONSTITUTION

With the country's political structure in flux, the street children's movement forged ahead. Movement leaders aimed at shaping a new constitution for the country. They envisaged a legal foundation for Brazil's democracy distinctive from the one that had governed the past. Children and adolescents had few rights and many handicaps. The movement would build intellectually on the International Declaration of the Rights of Children promulgated by the United Nations. First World countries pushed this declaration. Fitting in with the First World drew in Brazil's political leaders.

Brazilians in large numbers were working on the agenda, issue by issue. In addressing the street children issue, MNMMR served as the point of the lance in the mobilization to follow. MNMMR joined the National Conference of Brazilian Bishops, the National Front for the Defense of Child and Adolescent Rights, the National Order of

Attorneys, and other groups to form a loose and effective coalition. They aimed at mobilizing public opinion and at electing appropriate candidates to the assembly to write a new constitution. They pushed for a still wider coalition, this time seeking closer partnership with the government. Six government ministries joined with nongovernmental groups to form the National Commission on the Child and the Constitution.

Coalition leaders gained national attention for the initiative. In May 1986, they held the First National Meeting of Street Boys and Street Girls. Five hundred children and adolescents came as delegates from various corners of Brazil. The media featured the children and adolescents as speaking for themselves. The country was saturated with media coverage of the meeting.[23] In the last six months of 1986, the media ran almost 3,000 print articles and seventy-two television programs on children's rights.[24]

Massive mobilization followed. Two hundred thousand adults and 1.3 million children signed petitions favoring constitutional changes in favor of children's rights.[25] The process duly impressed members of the constitutional assembly, convened in 1988. The assembly approved the article covering children's rights the following year. Article 227 resembled the United Nation's International Convention.

However, observers believed general statements of rights had little worth. Brazil needed a delineation of rights expressed at length in a subsequent statute. Movement leaders set up, as objectives, educating a broad range of constituents and anticipating oppositional moves. They needed an even wider coalition of groups. Many nongovernmental organizations, within or outside MNMMR, pulled together into the Child and Adolescent Forum.

Framing Action

Next, movement leaders had to devise a national strategy. They lacked experience in democratic settings. However, they had at hand transnational mentors, such as United Nations advisers, to tutor them. Leaders looked over the modern repertoire of collective action. They chose public meetings and seminars as their instruments. They conducted thousands of meetings and seminars throughout a country larger than the continental United States. The meetings ostensibly sought public support for new and detailed legislation. However, the meetings also aimed at showing Brazilians the central place of rights and of the rule of law in democracy. They borrowed dominant themes (representation, sharing, and other democratic themes) used by Brazilian political parties. This repertoire rendered less effective the opposition of conservative political actors.

The media again played a vital role. Television, press, and radio gained attention for movement objectives. They also provided a diffuse vehicle for consensus formation. From a "correctional remedy" frame, they shifted the issue to "human rights." The movement brought about passage of key legislation. President Fernando Collor de Mello signed the Child and Adolescent Statute (with 267 articles) in July 1990.

The change of perspective between the old Minor's Code and the new Statute was radical.[26] Emphasis was placed on "child" and "adolescent" as categories referring to all Brazilians in certain age categories. In Brazil, rich people's offspring had been called children and adolescents. Poor offspring were called *meninos* (minors). Paul Jeffrey recalls a headline in Belém: "Minor Attacks Child," (a poor, thieving kid attacked a rich kid).[27] Doing away with *menino* in the Statute allowed emphasis on basic rights of children and youth as human beings. Given their vulnerabilities, young persons were accorded highest priority in policy considerations. Judges now could halt pork barrel projects until the state provided for the children's basic needs (such as elementary education).[28]

Institutional Inertia and Presidential Countermoves

The accomplishment of the movement—change in Constitution and establishment of Statute—was exemplary (human rights groups in other countries hoped to do the same), but, as opponents said, it was empty. They charged that the same machinery, people, and infrastructures were responsible locally for taking care of the children.

Violence by police and parapolice forces did not cease. Even the glare of international publicity was not strong enough to diminish its occurrence. For murders of children and adolescents in Río de Janeiro alone, the mass-circulation Brazilian newsmagazine *Istoe É* reported about 400 murders each year from 1990 to 1993.[29] Violence against children and adolescents seems to have diminished but still shocks foreigners.[30]

One might judge that the movement has been suitably tamed and rendered ineffectual by traditional political repertoires of the government. What was granted by the government under extreme pressure and public scrutiny were words and laws. These were nothing of grave consideration, especially for President Collor and associates. Patronage and cronyism quickly took hold in the "new" national politics of Brazil.

In effect, Presidents Collor and Itamar Franco (1990–1995) played an excellent political hand: they cooperated in a traditional decentralization-without-resources strategy. Proponents of change in the care of street children and adolescents argued for and were granted localized control. Few monies followed.

Further, powerholders within the political-bureaucratic apparatus carried on the authoritarian past. Eli Diniz and Renato Boschi pointed to features that persist: closed style, low transparency, little accountability, strong clientalistic ties, and low capacity for achievement and enforcement.[31]

Human rights activists faced not only strongly entrenched enclaves but also profound corruption of presidential power in Collor de Mello's administration. Inflated anticipation of the turn to democracy heightened the disappointments that followed. Grassroots activists, as from the base Christian communities, began saying, "A democracia e um engano" (Democracy is a deception).

Gains Made by Movement

Public pressure, fueled by human rights organizations, helped to bring down President Fernando Collor de Mello, as described in the chapter on corruption. Human rights groups, investigative reporters, and a host of other actors showed corrupt presidents could be rooted out. This small victory (the system remained in place) gave courage to human rights workers that presidential power did not confer absolute privilege.

In Brazil, many small steps at the municipal governmental level have taken effect. Here the interplay between nongovernmental and governmental actors continues as a political battleground. NGOs have wrested a measure of power in newly-created municipal councils in some cities. In many others, NGOs are ignored, held at arm's length, or their initiatives incorporated in local government programs for children where benign aspects of the program die.

Nonetheless, human rights activists point to a fundamental achievement: change in the law, by which they are willing to live and die. Willingness to trust the rule of law continues to drive human rights activists and marks a sea change in Brazilian and many Latin American societies.

Moreover, if a law is on the books, a good chance exists that public prosecutors will enforce the laws. As Dewees and Klees remark they do so "in part simply because the new law exists and their responsibility and personal orientation is to enforce laws."[32] Human rights activist lawyers, such as Sister Michael Mary Nolan, march on, presenting case after case, seeking justice for the killers of children. They helped to bring down a celebrated *justiciero* (vigilante), Cabo Bruno, a former policeman, who had bragged to the media about getting away with more than fifty killings.[33]

Advisers and educational consultants interviewed at United Nations Fund for Children (UNICEF) and the Inter-American Development Bank in Brasília believe that the Child and Adolescent laws are having a notable effect in Brazil.[34] They see an improvement on the streets in the treatment of children and adolescents by government agencies. Moreover, they point to the use of existing laws by parents to force school officials to respond to the needs of previously neglected children.

The laws provide political justification for creative programs to entice children to schools. The governor of the Federal District, a member of PT (Workers Party, supported by many churchmen), has devised a program to keep children off the streets and in school. Parents in dysfunctional families often use children as sources of income, keeping them out of schools. Further, Brazilian lower-class schools typically have rates of repeating grades as high as 70 percent. This waste greatly increases the cost of education. To remedy the situation, the governor's program provides parents with a month's minimum salary if students attend school daily. This has reduced nonattendance drastically.

Brazilian human rights activists are, in general, a hardy and inventive lot. They set up SOS telephone numbers for children and adolescents in peril. Institutions are beginning to provide training and help with income-earning opportunities. Many educators are training young people where they are, on the streets, in literacy and other basic skills. Persons and groups have responded by the thousands, to the extent that observers, like Duncan Green, believe that most children and adolescents have a place to go at night.[35]

CHILDREN AT RISK

Designating persons as street children came under heavy debate and fell into disuse in professional circles at the end of the 1990s, although street children continue to be discovered outside professional and academic circles. Catherine Panter-Brick notes a "sea-change" in studies concerning street youth. This occurred because the population is not homogeneous; does not correspond to the ways that many children relate their experiences or to the reality of their movements; is imbued with pitying connotations; and deflects attention from the broader population of children affected by social exclusion. In other words, it is better to move beyond a sole focus on the street.[36]

National efforts similar to Brazil and international efforts that resulted in the United Nations Convention on the Rights of the Child (1989) helped to change the conceptual framework about children in adversity. The change moved attention from needs to rights, as entitling them to the resources they require. Children are said to have three sets of rights: protection, provision, and participation. In the latter case, they are seen as having social agency and competency. Two major effects have followed this change. First, perspectives have changed to include those of children and, second, now embrace a wider universe of children at risk. This discourse may have leveled the field of attention so that children at home suffering abuse and neglect are also granted attention commensurate with those on the street.

CONCLUSION

Virtually all Latin American countries acquired an acute awareness of the problems of children at risk by the 1990s. Besides the gains noted in Brazil, contemporary efforts in Latin America, generally, to aid children at risk are making some progress. Very large efforts to aid children by government, international agencies, and grassroots efforts have provided these benefits. The Inter-American Development Bank turned from viewing inequality as an economic problem to funding projects to reduce social exclusion. UNICEF focused increasingly on children most at risk. Health organizations targeted children with the least access to health services. As a result, most children have a place to go at night. Informal and formal schooling opportunities have multiplied. In Brazil, in 2000, two-thirds of young people ages 17 to 20 have completed grade six, compared to less than half a decade ago. Poor children and adolescent's health is slowly improving.

Two countries on somewhat opposite ends of socioeconomic indexes, Mexico and Ecuador, have constructed a Child Rights Index, including the right to survival, the right to a healthy and safe environment, and the right to intellectual and emotional development. Mexico has shown a gradual improvement in the fulfillment of the rights of the country's children. The Index started at 4.68 in 1998, rose to 5.25 in 2001, and advanced to 5.71 in 2003. Ecuador's Index was created later than Mexico's, and it showed an overall improvement from 3.4 to 3.6 between 2002 and 2003.

NOTES

1. The story of one of the survivors who later hijacked a bus is told in the film *Bus 415*.
2. Paul Jeffrey, "Targeted for Death," *Christian Century* (Jan. 20, 1993): 155.
3. Besides Gilberto Dimenstein's *Brazil: The War on Children* (London: Latin America Bureau, 1991), see Elizabeth Hillman, "Some Hope for Brazil's Abandoned Children," *Contemporary Review* 264, 1539 (April 1994): 190–96.
4. Dimenstein, *Brazil:* vii.
5. For their history and methods, see Robert Gabriel Quinn, "The Reeducation and Rehabilitation of the Difficult Problem Girls under the Direction of the Sisters of Our Lady of Charity of the Good Shepherd of Angels," unpublished manuscript, Providence College Library, 1953.
6. Elizabeth Ann Kuznesof, "The House, The Street, and Global Society," *Journal of Social History* 38, 4 (2005): 859.
7. Kuznesof, *The House:* 860.
8. Carolina María de Jesus, *Child of the Dark* (various publishers, 1962 and ff.).
9. Tobias Hecht, *At Home in the Street: Street Children of Northeast Brazil* (New York: Cambridge, 1998): 81.
10. Hecht, *At Home:* 82.
11. Kuznesof, *The House:* 867.
12. For earlier history of voluntary organizations, see, for example: Alexandrina Sobreira de Moura, "Nongovernmental Organizations in Brazil: From Opposition to Partnership," paper for Latin American Studies International Congress, 1994.
13. Schneider, *Order and Progress: A Political History of Brazil* (Boulder: Westview, 1991): 264.
14. These changes were embodied in two major laws: The National Policy for the Welfare of Minors (PNEBEM) (1964) and the Minors Code (1979).
15. Anthony Dewees and Steven Klees, "Social Movements and the Transformation of National Policy: Street and Working Children in Brazil," *Comparative Education Review* 39, 1 (1995): 84.
16. See Nancy Scheper-Hughes and Daniel Hoffman, "Kids Out of Place," *NACLA Report on the Americas* 27, 6 (May–June 1994): 16–23, fn. 10.
17. Reported in Dimenstein, *Brazil:* 41.
18. UNICEF, *The State of the World's Children 1993* (New York: Oxford University Press, 1993): 38.
19. UNICEF, *State:* 38.
20. Entitled: First Latin American Seminar on Community Alternatives in Attention to Street Boys and Street Girls and held in November 1994.

21. Scheper-Hughes and Hoffman, "Kids": 16.

22. Costa, quoted in Anthony Swift, *The Fight for Childhood in the City* (Florence: UNICEF, 1991): 18.

23. Dewees and Klees, "Social Movements": 85.

24. UNICEF, *State:* 38.

25. For children's participation see: Steven Klees and Irene Rizzini "Child Rights and Children's Involvement in the Making of a New Constitution in Brazil," *Cultural Survival Quarterly* (Summer 2000).

26. Dewees and Klees, "Social Movements": 87ff.

27. Jeffrey, "Targeted": 158.

28. Innovations of content, methods, and decision making in the Statute are considered by Dewees and Klees, "Social Movements": 88–89.

29. *Isto É* 1243 (June 28, 1993): 16.

30. See endnote 35.

31. Diniz and Boschi, "A consolidacão democrática no Brasil: Atores políticos, processos sociais e intermediacãco de interesses," in Diniz, Boschi, and Renato Lessa, *Modernizacão e consolidacão democrática no Brasil: Dilemas da Nova República* (São Paulo: Ediçaos Vétice, 1989): 58–59.

32. Dewees and Klees, "Social Movements": 91.

33. "Getting Away with Murder," CBS News *Sixty Minutes*, Dec. 1, 1991.

34. Interviews, Brasília, May 30, 1996.

35. Interview, London, Dec. 14, 1995. Green conducted a survey of children in several countries. See his *Hidden Lives: Voices of Children in Latin America and the Caribbean* (Washington, DC: Cassell, 1998).

36. Lord David Alton, a member of the British upper chamber, wished to continue special efforts focused on street children. In 2004, he effectively burst into public attention with the program Stop Killing Children—Jubilee Campaign. An all-party alliance, Lords and Commons, formed to sponsor the campaign. Representatives from parties and the government met in the crowded Jubilee Room of the House of Commons to launch a website stopkillingchildren.com. The website focused then on killings of children in Brazil but was to be extended worldwide. By early 2006, the effort was floundering.

4

Indigenous Rights Resurgence

After centuries of living on the margins of society, indigenous peoples pushed their way not only into public consciousness but also into Congress and the presidential palace. This occurred in Bolivia, the most Indian state, but advances have been made elsewhere. After the long history of exclusion from most of the seats of power in the country, by the 1990s Indian men and women began to be seated in Congress. By 2006, Evo Morales Ayma ascended from Congress to the presidency of the country. He was not the first Indian to be elected president of a Latin American country. Next door, in Peru, Alejandro Toledo had that honor, but Dr. Toledo, with a Stanford Ph.D., had no substantial indigenous base, whereas Morales was a man with large segments of the indigenous movement behind him.

In many countries Indians have moved to center stage of politics. Indigenous rights reached the top of the human rights agenda. The indigenous movement became the region's strongest political movement of the 1990s. These advances could not have been predicted in 1980. Then, as noted in previous chapters, the military was leaving the presidency in various countries of Latin America, and the focus was on forging democratic states from authoritarian regimes. Human rights groups had been fully occupied with dealing with death, disappearance, torture, and imprisonment. Then, in some token or real way, national governments dealt with accounting for the past. Bolivia was one of the first to attempt to account for its past, though not thoroughly. Much later, Peru, another country with a large indigenous population, created an exemplary Commission for Truth and Reconciliation. This commission proved important for also establishing the truth about discrimination against its indigenous population and massive rights violations.

The following sections discuss, first, indigenous peoples, state policy, and contemporary awakenings. The second section addresses the demands the movements have made and transnational human rights networks. The third section assesses the contemporary situation of indigenous issues, focusing on land issues.

MOBILIZATIONS, POPULATIONS, AND STATE POLICY

Human rights groups were tardy in urging indigenous organizations to come forward to claim their rights. Indigenous people were invisible, or they were expected to claim their rights as individual citizens, not as a collective group. Indigenous peoples came forward from their own inner impulse, implanted through education and nurture. For those who had viewed Latin America's indigenous as passive peasants, the indigenous national marches in Ecuador and Bolivia in 1990 were stunning developments.

In this awakening to their cultural rights, indigenous peoples were aided by foreign and national anthropologists and Catholic and Protestant missionaries. Indigenous movements would not have appeared as readily or in the form in which they appeared without outside help. The impulse to organize and to act in the public sphere in new ways came in large part from these outside sources.[1]

Contemporary Awakenings

The first notable indigenous movement appeared in Ecuador. The political assertiveness of the Shuar peoples, supported by Salesian missionaries, began in the early 1960s. Their activism spread to peoples of the neighboring Peruvian Amazon region. The first Peruvian congress of indigenous, Congreso Amuesha, took place in 1968. This was followed by the formation of the Council of Aguarana and Huambisha and then the Front for the Defense of the Native Shipibo Communities. By the beginning of the 1980s, the three groups had pulled together into the Interethnic Association for the Development of the Peruvian Jungle (AIDESEP). The group went on to become the principal voice of the eastern Peruvian Indians. Similar grassroots stirrings were occurring in southern Mexico, Guatemala, and Bolivia.

These were the behind-the-scenes activities. Three large public events in Latin America received global attention and shook nations that were largely unprepared for challenges the indigenous made. A 1990 march in Ecuador brought the nation to a halt. In the same year in Bolivia, lesser-known Indians from the eastern part of the country conducted a national march across the country, called the March for Territory and Dignity, but the event that captured the most attention was the Chiapas uprising. In the southern Mexico state of Chiapas, Indians led by Subcomandante Marcos rose in armed revolt against the state on New Year's Eve 1994 to protest the signing of the North American Free Trade Agreement (NAFTA) with the United States and Canada. Another striking event occurred in 2000 in Ecuador. After widespread demonstrations to make their demands clear, Ecuadorian Indians forged an alliance with a sector of the military, and together they took over the Congress building, an event that ended with the ouster of President Jamil Mahaud.

These and other events that occurred between 1990 and 2000 showed a widespread and easily ignited indigenous activism. The focal point for energizing Latin

America's Indians was debate surrounding the Fifth Centenary of Columbus's and the Spaniards' arrival in Santo Domingo that was to be celebrated in 1992.[2] Because the debate involved Europe, the United Nations and European capitals also were drawn-in to the discussion. Prolonged preparations for celebrating these historical milestones gave indigenous peoples and a wide public audience the opportunity to discuss nationally and internationally the negative as well as the positive aspects of colonization.

Through all these events, indigenous people made clear that they would no longer accept their subordinate status. Two sets of demands were being made. The first were the commonly understood human rights, and the second were collective rights, to be taken up later. In the first set of rights, the indigenous were largely excluded from education, occupational advancement, and health care. Further, they were afflicted with the injustice of active discrimination. Latin America was a deeply racist society.

Indigenous movements were impelled in part by recent memories of extreme levels of hatred in Guatemala and Peru where state-sponsored killings of the indigenous took place during civil wars. The Peruvian Commission for Truth and Reconciliation found that 70,000 died or disappeared during the government's war against guerrilla forces, such as the Sendero Luminoso. The indigenous were the main victims. Seventy-five percent of victims were Indians, mostly Quechua-speakers. While Senderistas killed 54 percent of the indigenous victims, Peru's security forces killed or disappeared 46 percent, a remarkably high percentage. The report showed the depth of racial discrimination and the high degree of vulnerability of the rural indigenous population.

In Guatemala, three commissions uncovered killings of indigenous that came close to genocide. Christian Tomuschat, chair of the UN-sponsored National Commission for Historical Clarification, delivered the commission's report in a solemn act at the National Theater. He said that the killings, at the level of genocide, were carried out by agents of the state against the Mayan people. Most of the 200,000 persons who died or disappeared from 1954 until 1996 were indigenous.

He added that "The Mayan population paid the highest price for the irrational logic of the armed conflict. . . . In various parts of the country, the military identified groups of Mayan people as natural allies of the guerrillas. This fact is evidenced by the aggressive, racist, and extremely cruel nature of the violations of the massive extermination of defenseless Mayan communities."

Indigenous Populations

Indigenous people number about thirty-five to forty million persons in Latin America. That number amounts to about 8–10 percent of the total population of the region. However, since most indigenous live in the region of the old Inca or Mayan civilizations, they are found primarily in Ecuador, Peru, Bolivia, Guatemala, and Mexico. Percentages of Indians range from 70 percent in Bolivia to 15 percent in Mexico. Nonetheless, Mexico has twelve million indigenous. This compares with about two million indigenous in all of the United States and Canada. (Brazil receives a great deal of attention for its Indians, but they are a tiny fraction of the total population.) Diversity of language and culture marks all the Indian countries. Mexico has more than fifty indigenous languages. Guatemala has at least twenty-two language and cultural groups. In the Andean countries, similar diversity can be found in the lowlands.

The Indian populations have been formed by centuries of accommodations to geography and environment. Geography determined the ecological conditions that serve as the economic basis of life and culture for the indigenous peoples. Neither Indian life in the Americas nor their political demands can be understood without an understanding of their natural environment, especially their relationship to their land to which they are deeply bound and which is considered sacred.

In South America, anthropologists found the greatest differences in environment and Indian culture between highland and lowland Indians. By far, the larger number of Indians lived in the mountains and their valleys. The cooler climate and somewhat greater ease in transportation provided the conditions for agricultural surplus, storage, and communication between settlements. Economic surplus brought about economic classes, intellectual and ruling elites, and conditions for a more sophisticated culture. Higher technology and a measure of scientific achievement, as in astronomy and mathematics, followed. The Inca and other civilizations left cultural heritages in South America, as did the Mayan, Zapotec, and other civilizations in Guatemala-Chiapas and southern Mexico. Among deeply-held beliefs that are core to indigenous peoples and their political demands are community and respect for elders and tradition.

Indigenous now live in cities and urban areas in great numbers, although one has to recognize the great fluidity of movement between *campo* and city. Further, indigenous live in some large cities as indigenous, in parallel lives with mestizo and European counterparts. However, the majority of Indians are found in areas dominated by rural agriculture. These regions, as the Andean and Guatemalan altiplanos, tend to suffer from high poverty rates, slim access to health, education, and social services, and frequent conflicts over labor rights and land resources. Since the late 1960s, a combination of population growth, land consolidation, and civil unrest has both fueled migration and increased the difficulties of eking a living from nearly exhausted soils. Globalization of agriculture with large landholdings have greatly affected traditional farmers, reducing landholdings, making competition almost impossible, and increasing the price of commodities one might wish to consume, such as beef. From Mexico to Chile, the social and economic effects of structural adjustment in the 1980s and neo-liberal economic policies in the 1990s left indigenous populations especially vulnerable and less connected to their communities of origin. The Zapatista rebellion in Chiapas was a cry from the heart about miseries increased by global forces now impinging on those living on the margins of national and global society.

The definition of who is an Indian has changed over time. The majority of Indians in Peru and Bolivia became *campesinos* (peasants) in the mid-twentieth century, as a more honored term. *Indio* was reserved for people who lived in the forests and jungle areas of the eastern parts of the countries. In Paraguay, the majority of citizens are of Guaraní descent and speak the language, so the term *indio* is used for people who live communally in remote areas. Bolivia's ethnic majority groups, Aymara and Quechua, chose to move back to the usage of *indio* for themselves in the 1970s. This was a powerful statement of their identity. It was also a statement of their intention to push Bolivia toward acceptance of a pluralist society, in which *indios* would have an honored place as part of the ancient heritage of the country. They would also be recognized as bearers of collective rights that existed before the Spanish or Bolivian states existed.

In the 1960s and 1970s, since many indigenous were living in two worlds, rural and urban, social scientists used language (what language was spoken at home) and dress (western or Indian) as major indicators of identity. Census-takers and social scientists later switched to self-identification. The author here adopts a broader definition of indigenous as a person who identifies him or herself as part of a group distinct from dominant society, with connections to precolonial society, and an interest in preserving elements and practices of ethnic identity.[3]

All the five Indian countries have had a so-called "Indian problem" through their histories. Often this was framed in terms of assimilation and integration. Indians would have to fit into efforts at nation-building, a process that has gone on since independence from Spain (1810–1825). Political elites believed that Indians were better left uneducated until progressive elites in the 1920s thought they needed to have some primary schooling and to learn Spanish to unify the country. Typically, schools were the instruments of integration whereby indigenous children were taught in Spanish and penalized for speaking native languages. Their own cultures were ignored or deprecated by schools and teachers as backward whereas the nation, through its schools, was heading toward modernity.

Indigenous Resurgence and Religion

Counterforces against these policies were at work in Latin America.[4] The indigenous were forming their own ideology that placed a high value on cultural rights and that would pose a direct challenge to *indigesimo*. Rodolfo Stavenhagen and others have noted that Indians could only be making this challenge with the aid of outside support. The chief institutions fostering this process were Catholic and Protestant missions. The acknowledgment by anthropologists and others social scientists of this religious support is a turnaround from the accusations made by anthropologists after World War II that missionaries were holding back the political development of indigenous peoples.

As leading authorities on Indians in Latin America highlighted their political activism, they also alluded to the religious basis of this movement without directly investigating it. The field remained open for investigation. Alison Brysk, in the best account of Indian movements as a transnational enterprise, found that liberation theology

"played a critical role in establishing indigenous movements and remains a key refer-
ent in areas."[5] According to Brysk, "concerned clergy were the most frequent (and periodically successful) interlocutors for Indian interests" in Latin America.[6] The wider
task of tracing the influence of religious groups in national contexts was undertaken in
a 2005 publication. *Resurgent Voices in Latin America: Indigenous Peoples, Political
Mobilization, and Religious Change* was published as a collaborative effort to delineate
the history of the religious impulse for activism.[7] Religion within Indian movements is
important for major reasons. One cannot understand Indian insurgency or Latin
America without recourse to religious explanations. Religion forms a major component
of indigenous life and culture. Further, Indian religion is enlivening the Catholic and
Protestant national churches in Latin America, some of them major players in politics
in Latin America. Lastly, some forms of Indian religion—non-Christian forms—challenge both Catholic and Protestant Christian churches.

Within social science and theology, a notable shift has taken place to include culture, including ethnic identity and religion as a major components of analysis. Darren
Sherkat and Christopher Ellison note that "religious beliefs, commitments, and resources are an important part of building and maintaining ethnic identities and they
provide the ideological and actual resources brought to bear in ethnic conflicts."[8]

As in the civil rights movement in the sixties or among some African-American
churches since that time, religion served as a versatile fuel for mobilization. Religious
ideologies provided a groundwork for the framing of movement issues. Religious institutions enhanced the acceptance of movement positions, provided social legitimacy,
and helped to ward off repression. Furthermore, as a number of Latin American scholars, such as Daniel Levine and Anna Peterson, have noted, religion furnished narratives
for movements, providing a rationale for action and a foundation for collective identities and group solidarity.[9]

One of the critical moments for change occurred in 1971. That year the Barbados
Conference of the International Work Group for Indigenous Affairs[10] charged that governments, international agencies, and missionaries were participating in programs of
ethnocide.[11] While the charges were leveled specifically about non-Andean Indians,
the implications reached to include relations generally with missionaries, the churches,
and indigenous peoples.

Changes in indigenous policy were taking place in the churches, so the Barbados
conference served as a further wake-up call for them. The conference also helped to
launch the international indigenous rights movement.[12] Anthropologists and indigenous activists at that meeting established themselves as catalysts for a transnational
movement. Their activities opened up an era of globalized actions in relation to the
nation-state and Indian rights movements. In part as a response to Barbados, religious
institutions played a critical role in this process. In the last third of the twentieth century, some religious bodies responded extensively to the perceived need to aid tribal
leaders in organizing to pressure governments for their rights and privileges as full

citizens. The World Council of Churches throughout the 1970s flew Indian leaders to regional meetings. Between 1970 and 1981 the Brazilian Catholic bishops sponsored fifteen meetings, bringing together hundreds of indigenous leaders from about 200 groups. From these international conferences to local assets provided through religious organizations, the critical networks, resources, and ideological frameworks for Latin America's indigenous resurgence were formed.

Major shifts in policy and religious thought and action were spurred and supported by major changes within the institutional Catholic Church. The general thrust of Vatican Council II (1962–1965) included two key factors that would affect Latin America: adaptation of a universal church to national and local cultures and awareness of the presence of God in other religions (such as that of Latin America's indigenous).

The Medellín Conference of Latin American Bishops (CELAM) in 1968 reinforced these trends, emphasizing the "Latin Americanization" of the church. Changes in attitude toward the indigenous became inevitable. Inculturation, the process of discerning where God is at work in a culture and articulating a theology sensitive to the local context, became the aim of church leaders and theologians. To summarize, CELAM changed its policy toward the indigenous from indigenista to indígena, from paternalistic to accompaniment in the 1970s and 1980s.[13] In its most specific form, guidelines for this indigenism included: (1) defending the land; (2) learning the indigenous languages; (3) motivating self-determination; (4) equipping the community for contact with outsiders; (5) recovering cultural memory; (6) providing hope; and (7) stimulating alliances.[14]

Liberation theology also emerged in Latin America in the 1960s as a way of proposing that the church, as a people and an institution, exert an active role in society. This way of thinking contrasted with the Latin American Catholic Church's previous role as an otherworldly, fiesta-bound institution. Liberation theology centered its concerns in a preferential option for the poor, weak, and vulnerable. Its theologians advocated social change, action to promote justice, and emphasized small communities with lay and clerical leadership as the basis of action.

Liberation theology can claim two important contributions to present-day theologizing throughout the world: method and context. Both are salient here. Liberation theologians emphasized an inductive method: begin with a description of the world and the church within it, reflect on the situation from a Biblical perspective, and act to bring the world and the church more in harmony with this Biblical vision. Liberation theology also took the lead in what is today called contextual theology.[15] This contextual theology attempts to express Christian faith in distinct languages, thought patterns, and other cultural expressions.

A number of missionaries in Bolivia, Peru, and elsewhere in Latin America also began to develop a theological perspective with a greater focus on the value of local culture. In this view, culture has the central position for description and explanation. Early forms of liberation theology were seen as ignoring culture, emphasizing the strictly socioeconomic aspects of Latin America. Further, culturalists believed that the liberationist perspective may have brought failure to many indigenous development projects because the projects were based on socioeconomic analysis that excluded cultural factors. Some members of this sector also saw liberation theology as looking for a socialist world that never came.[16] In the end, both liberationists and culturalists helped to foster the growth of indigenous theologians, who would eventually bring about a fuller elaboration of *teología india*.[17]

Key to indigenous movements has been the role of religious education. The Adventists built many schools around Lake Titicaca that separates Bolivia and Peru. These schools produced graduates who went on to fill local and national leadership roles. Catholic seminaries trained indigenous and nonindigenous priests who, in turn, trained catechists who would later go on to become community leaders and key organizers in indigenous social movements. In Guatemala, the individuals trained under Catholic Action came to represent a new generation of leadership in indigenous communities. Some Protestant pastors, especially Mayan Presbyterian pastors, emerged as local and national indigenous leaders of the Mayan movement.

However, the most direct linking of religion and cultural awareness took place in important national and regional centers that were devoted to study, research, and informal education of indigenous leaders. Seven important centers were created for this purpose in Peru and Bolivia, anchored by the Catholic universities in Lima and Cochabamba. Similar indigenous cultural or human rights centers were established in Alto Verapaz in Guatemala and San Cristóbal de Las Casas in Chiapas. Probably the most prominent of all the centers, National Center for Aid to Indigenous Missions (CENAMI), was created in Mexico City. These centers were closely linked with the education of catechists. Several hundred thousand of the 1.1 million catechists in the Latin American church are indigenous and many serve as community leaders, as well as being in Andrew Orta's assessment "vernacular intellectuals," persons who interpret the Christian message within a specific culture. In addition to religious education, many catechists worked on two tasks. They helped raise political consciousness in indigenous communities and they encouraged indigenous to organize to struggle for their own rights. They conceived this as the self-emanicipation of the poor.[18]

Virtually all sectors of public life—intellectuals, political parties, public officials, and state bureaucrats—discouraged politicized indigenous identification until the 1980s and 1990s when indigenous began to take things into their own hands. Guillermo de la Peña, a Mexican scholar, has carefully traced the trajectory of social and cultural policies toward indigenous peoples in Latin America. He summarizes these policies as based on *indigenismo*, "an ideological movement that denounced the exploitation of aboriginal groups and strove for the cultural unity and the extension of citizenship through social integration and acculturation."[19] Lands that were distributed and services, such as health, were also tools for governing and controlling. Indigenist policies were related to populist tendencies in most Latin American countries and when these countries became newly democratic and tried to fit into free-market capitalism, a neoliberal discourse prevailed, one that allowed for an opening to multiculturalism.

DEMANDS AND TRANSNATIONAL NETWORKS

Indigenous intellectuals and indigenous movements denounced indigenist policies. The author was editing *Estudios Andinos* from La Paz, Bolivia, at the time and was privileged to know the persons who put forward one of the first such statements of denunciation. A core group of Aymara intellectuals, the Katarists, appeared dramatically on the public stage at Tiahuanaco, the premier indigenous site in Bolivia, with a carefully crafted statement called the Tiahuanaco Manifesto in 1973. Cultural assimilation and education exclusively in the Spanish language were all condemned.[20] Due to the military dictatorship in power when the Manifesto was "announced" in the Latin American fashion, the national media paid little attention. With the help of the progressive Catholic Church and some clandestine groups, the Manifesto received serious attention at the grassroots.

A few years later, with state authoritarian controls diminishing, the Jesuit priest Xavier Albó helped young Aymara leaders found the Tupac Katari Center that fostered an enlarged Katarista movement. Within a relatively brief time the movement took over most of the official government peasant unions and organized its own union. Aymaras asserted themselves with a degree of political sophistication and independence not seen since colonial times. They also broadened the labor movement to bring together urban and mine workers with rural workers. They had a much larger target, though, than labor rights. They took aim at the state, presenting their demands about unequal treatment from the state for agricultural prices, credit, education, and health. They proposed a series of revindications about the nature of ethnicity and the basic racial definitions of national society. The Katarists helped move what had been in Bolivia a cultural awareness movement to one with political goals.

Identity politics now became the common way of describing what was taking place. The 1994 uprising in Chiapas confirmed a shift from national-popular revolution that dominated much of twentieth-century Latin American political ideology, as that of the Sandinistas in Nicaragua. Indians mobilized because of their distinctively indigenous identity. As Charles Hale notes: "Indigenous peoples now increasingly advance their struggles through a discourse that links Indian identity with rights to territory, autonomy, and peoplehood—rights that run parallel to those of the nation-state itself."[21]

As indigenous intellectuals, centers, and movements took shape, they enunciated these political goals: self-determination and autonomy, cultural distinctiveness not cultural integration, political reforms, including changes in constitutions, territorial rights and access to natural resources, and reforms of military and police powers in relation to the indigenous.

Overlooked by a number of analysts exploring the larger goals of indigenous movements in the 1990s was local indigenous activism in all but Guatemala (where a civil war was tearing apart large sectors of the indigenous and ladino populations) in the 1970s and 1980s. This activism was aimed at adult literacy, primary and secondary education, and improvement of health. This activism paid off splendidly. In basic areas of education and health some spectacular gains have been made. The most basic skill that was lacking in the indigenous population was literacy. This has notably improved so that South America had a 90 percent literacy rate in 2002, with Central America and the Caribbean standing at 87 percent. This is far ahead of Sub-Saharan Africa's 63 percent and Asia's 74 percent. In times past, the Indian countries of Latin America lagged behind the countries without large indigenous populations. Gains in youth literacy, presumably from formal schooling, from 1990 to 2001, were exemplary in the five Indian countries. Health conditions improved generally in the late twentieth century among Latin Americans and the indigenous shared in some of the gains. Using underweight prevalence in children under five as an indicator, in 1995–2002, South America had 6 percent; Central America and the Caribbean 10 percent to Asia's 30 percent and Sub-Saharan Africa's 31 percent.[22]

The indigenous movements in Bolivia and elsewhere were both helped and hindered by established political parties. These parties fostered remarkable changes in constitutions and in public policies but represented many other interests than indigenous ones. The older parties also were perceived as favoring economic policies that benefited the elite, to the detriment of the poor and marginal peoples. One of the crucial conflicts in Bolivia came over a water supply contract awarded with approval of legislative bodies run by older political parties to the Bechtel Corporation. Indigenous activists made an issue of Bolivians paying foreigners for the use of their own national resources. The indigenous led the successful fight against ruling elites to void the contract. In a word, both parties and governmental institutions had fundamental problems of representation. As Robert Barr has commented: "Representative institutions have not fully responded to the new pluralistic landscape, despite a range of political reforms."[23] Bolivia has seen an almost continuous cycle of protest from 1999. Bolivians, Barr believes, turn to protest because they do not trust formal means of representation. Further, Indian movements in Bolivia took the drastic step of creating their own political parties from scratch. Evo Morales won the presidency with his Movement Toward Socialism (MAS).[24]

What was becoming evident was that Indians no longer depended largely on outsiders as their interlocutors with larger society. Pan-Mayanism, the Kataristas, and other Indian movements had their own public intellectuals. Indians were beginning to speak for themselves, although unwilling to cast entirely free from their mentors.

Transnational Movement

That these movements formed part of a transnational movement also became clearer in the 1990s. A few prescient observers moved from writing about the big story of human rights movements that heroically opposed military dictatorships in Latin America to the relatively unknown story of Indians on the periphery of society seeking their rights. Alison Brysk led the way. She had framed in 1994 one of the most careful and acclaimed analyses of the Argentine human rights situation.[25] She then turned to the Indian rights movements.[26]

Through a series of publications ending in her masterful *From Tribal Village to Global Village: Indian Rights and International Relations in Latin America*, Brysk showed the impact of Indian rights movements on world politics.[27] Indian movements helped to reform the United Nations in its policies, to strengthen international law regarding minority rights, and to control the reach of transnational corporations into Indian domains. She argued that marginalized Indians have responded to globalization with new, internationalized forms of identity politics that are reconstructing power relations.

In doing so, Brysk traced a wide dynamics of interstate relations, global markets and transnational civil society. Others, such as Donna Van Cott, explored the implications of Indian activism for the new democracies of Latin America formed after military rule. Societies where Indians had large numbers could not simply go back to the same power relations that existed before military government. Indians will not let them. (This is a continuing story.) Looking at Guatemala and the Central Andes in 1998, John Peeler concluded that "the last generation has seen an unprecedented emergence of indigenous people as mainstream actors."[28] Xavier Albó, Deborah Yashar, Christian Gros, Donna Van Cott, Rachel Sieder, David Maybury-Lewis, Kay Warren and Jean Jackson, Ronald Niezen, Frank Salomon, Stuart Schwartz, and their colleagues have shown an evolution of contemporary state politics and new policy outcomes forged in conflict by Indian activists.[29]

A wide array of transnational organizations has influenced changes of states and economies. The International Monetary Fund and the World Bank, backed by the G7 nations, applied extreme pressure on Latin American states to resolve fiscal and governability crises by adopting what Latin Americans called neoliberal reforms to promote democracy and opening of markets in nations in the 1980s. First, more political space was allowed for political activity by citizens at the grassroots once authoritarian controls lessened. The neoliberal emphasis on decentralization of the state has led to devolution of power to more local units. This allowed indigenous groups to argue for greater indigenous local autonomy, as well. Indigenous organizations are thus armed with a dual logic for mobilization, calling their governments to task for failure to guarantee individual rights while demanding recognition and legal status for their group and ethnic identities.

However, the states that emerged from authoritarian governance attempted economic reforms that fell heavily on the poor and especially the indigenous peoples. The reforms were stabilization and structural adjustment programs, programs advocated by the agents of a globalized economy, such as the International Monetary Fund, World Bank, and Inter-American Development Bank. Newly democratic governments advanced neoliberal reforms by reducing budgets for agriculture, education, health and other social services, and programs of protecting peasant lands, access to credit, and agricultural subsidies. In sum, the indigenous faced diminishing resources from the state while real wage income in the agricultural sector from the 1980s decreased 30 percent by 1992.[30]

In contrast to diminished help from the state, transnational NGOs and international organizations such as the United Nations have been crucial in applying pressure on states to recognize cultural groups and their rights as part of neoliberalism and diversity. Indigenous activists found support for their agenda in key international institutions. The International Labour Organization's (ILO) Convention 169 commits those states that sign it to ensure the economic, cultural, labor, and land rights of indigenous people. Along with the United Nations and the Organization of American States Draft Declaration on Indigenous Rights, ILO Convention 169 spurred a series of constitutional reforms recognizing the multicultural nature of Latin American societies.

The larger world of global trade threatened Indian culture. Indians responded with many of the same tools as global traders. When Subcomandante Marcos and his companions rose up in Chiapas, e-mails were streaming from their headquarters to friends, protectors, and collaborators in Mexico City, Minneapolis, and Boston. When Ecuadoran Indians took up defense of their cause they did so in New York and Geneva conference rooms, as well as in Quito. The categories of "traditional" [used for indigenous culture] and "modern" dissolved when one encountered native persons who were transnationalized, urban, proletarian, border-crossing, trilingual, and computer-adept.[31]

Indigenous activists found in the United Nations an especially strong ally. This development is reflected in the establishment of the Working Group on Indigenous Populations (WGIP) in 1982, the proclamation by the United Nations General Assembly of the International Decade for Indigenous Peoples, 1995–2004, and the establishment of the Permanent Forum on Indigenous Issues in 2000.

CONTEMPORARY ASSESSMENT AND THE LAND ISSUE

Given the rough debates in the United States about the United Nations and the characterizations of the United Nations by Ambassador John Bolton, it may be difficult for North Americans to believe that the United Nations has done anything worthwhile regarding human rights. In fact, the office of the High Commissioner for Human Rights, based in Geneva, Switzerland, has been crucial in the continuing fight in the

2000s for implementation of the gains made in constitutions and laws that benefit indigenous peoples. In 2001, the UN Commission on Human Rights within the office of the High Commissioner appointed Rodolfo Stavenhagen from Mexico as Special Rapporteur on the situation of human rights and fundamental freedoms of indigenous people. This was done in response to the growing international concern regarding the marginalization and discrimination against indigenous people worldwide. Stavenhagen is regarded as a Great Man in anthropological circles with dozens of books and articles dealing with the indigenous and their rights. These are less important now that his views expressed since the 1960s are largely incorporated into various states' legislation than his contemporary efforts to act as intermediary and catalyst as states increasingly neglect demands and rights of their indigenous. Stavenhagen has visited countries, like Bolivia, reinforcing the views of the indigenous on complex issues, such as the selling of natural resources to foreign owners. His most important contribution may be his annual reports delivered with the authority of respected expertise. In 2003, he called attention to the impact of major development projects in areas occupied by the indigenous. He pointed out that indigenous communities will undergo profound social and economic changes that are not well-understood, much less foreseen by the authorities and agents promoting them.

In 2004, he addressed the issue of the administration of justice and indigenous peoples. From information received from many regions and sources, he concluded that the indigenous continue as victims of perennial prejudice and discrimination. Even when protective legislation is available, indigenous rights are frequently denied in practice. These findings are not new. What is new is that the indigenous found a voice in international circles, a voice that is strong and trustworthy.

Stavenhagen's findings were reinforced by Amnesty International. Ten years after the Fifth Columbus Centenary (1992), AI reported that the indigenous remain among the most maginalized and poorest communities, discriminated against and often exposed to grave abuses of their fundamental rights. This, the organization said, was in contrast to more than half the countries on the continent recognizing the multicultural character of the state and despite the guarantee of rights in constitutions and legislation. There does not appear to be a sufficient reason for this continued discrimination.

Land and Conflicts

By contrast, indigenous land rights are another story, with many legitimate claims in conflict. To summarize the background of the issue, first, as noted, anthropologists have been strongly involved in fostering indigenous consciousness and in supporting their rights. Individual anthropologists, such as Charles Wagley and David Mayberry-Lewis, some fifty years ago focused on the survival of Amazonian cultures in the face of various forces determined to develop the region. NGOs formed to help the indigenous have been gaining strength since those beginnings. Mayberry-Lewis and associates have been devoted to land and allied issues since the founding of Cultural Survival in 1971. Second, Convention 169 of the ILO, mentioned previously, was a major turning point from an assimilationist to an autonomous viewpoint. For the first time it used the term *territory* to refer to indigenous traditional landholding. This was defined as the total environment the indigenous occupy or otherwise use. Further specifications were mandated to facilitate indigenous peoples' possession and use. It is noteworthy that many Latin American states signed the document while almost no state outside Latin America has signed. Third, the biodiversity movement took shape in the 1980s and exerted considerable influence with national governments and international bodies. Within the biodiversity movement, scholars and activists believed that indigenous peoples were the best guardians of the land.

However, land rights policy seems impossible to implement. Briefly stated, Anthony Stocks characterizes a major part of this problem as too much land for too few people.[32] Positively, his survey of research shows that the indigenous struggle to regain control over lands is viewed as legitimate and legal and that the World Bank has been a leader in keeping pressure on the politicians. However, "the bad news is that the squatters, gold miners, ranchers, guerrillas, local police forces, paramilitaries, oil companies, loggers, and assorted claimants to space and resources occupied by indigenous people have not gotten the message."[33]

Thus, the political opening that incipient democracy afforded indigenous people to contest the state also brought in other actors with similar desires. In looking carefully at several countries, Stocks found that nonindigenous sectors have contested indigenous land titling and made it difficult to control even titled lands. "The forward movement with regard to indigenous lands is in real danger of being contested so sharply and powerfully that it will effectively be extinguished. Sometimes the men with the guns just take what they want," Stocks concluded.[34] He sees the future as a challenge for indigenous groups to improve their own organizations, for NGOs to concentrate on land issues and to support and to link with government agencies with a mandate to apply indigenous land laws. By contrast to those hopeful possibilities, the fundamental problem is that Latin American states have grown weak in the central exercise of power. Indigenous victories about land appear to be "Pyrrhic," or Stavenhagen may be correct in his assessment that the indigenous and their allies are just at the beginning of an arduous battle to regain sacred territories.

CONCLUSION

The indigenous mobilizations led to new constitutional provisions for Indian rights in Colombia and Bolivia. Van Cott has shown in her *The Friendly Liquidation of the Past: The Politics of Diversity in Latin America* that Indian activism led to constitutional reforms that espoused a more local, participatory, and culturally diverse society.[35] Both countries have created multicultural constitutional frameworks that recognize customary law, collective property rights, and bilingual education. Other countries—Guatemala, Nicaragua, Mexico, Argentina, Brazil, Paraguay, Ecuador, and Venezuela—with strong indigenous influence have granted important concessions that redefine the state and Indian groups.[36] However, the fight is far from over, as statutes mean little in practice without further political pressure. Further, substantial legislation with enforcement policies has yet to be created in Mexico and Guatemala, with almost half the Indians of Latin America. Only a noteworthy start in a long and painful conflict has begun there.

NOTES

1. Among the external sources, missionaries are most commonly cited. See, for example: Alison Brysk, *From Tribal Village to Global Village*, passim, and Rodolfo Stavenhagen, "Indigenous Organizations": 70.

2. The Fifth Centenary of Brazil's occupation by the Portuguese was 2000, not 1992.

3. This is in conformity with UN policy on defining indigenous.

4. Rodolfo Stavenhagen, Indigenous Organizations: Rising Actors in Latin America *CEPAL Review* 62 (August 1997): 63.

5. Alison Brysk, *From Tribal Village to Global Village: Indian Rights and International Relations in Latin America* (Stanford, CA: Stanford University Press, 2000): 194.

6. Ibid., 9.

7. Edward L. Cleary and Timothy J. Steigenga, eds., *Resurgent Voices in Latin America* (New Brunswick, NJ: Rutgers University Press, 2005).

8. Darren E. Sherkat and Christopher B. Ellison, "Recent Developments and Current Controversies in the Sociology of Religion," *Annual Review of Sociology* 25 (1999): 369.

9. This has been a consistent theme in Daniel Levine's influential work. See esp. his *Popular Voices in Latin American Catholicism* (Princeton, NJ: Princeton University Press, 1992). Anna Peterson, *Martyrdom and the Politics of Religion: Progressive Catholicism in El Salvador's Civil War* (Albany, NY: State University of New York Press, 1997).

10. See Miguel Alberto Bartolomé, *Declaration of Barbados* (Rooseveltown, NY: International Work Group for Indigenous Affairs, 1971).

11. The role of the World Council of Churches in the Declaration of Barbados and the evolution of anthropologists' views, as those of Guillermo Bonfil, are detailed by Andrew Walls and Lannin Senneh in their Prospectus for the 11th Yale-Edinburgh Group on Non-Western Christianity, July 12–14 meeting at New Haven.

12. The second Barbados Conference of the International Work Group for Indigenous Affairs took place in 1977 and issued a revised declaration signed by Indian representatives as well as anthropologists.

13. See esp. Consejo Episcopal Latinoamericano, *De una pastoral indigenista a una pastoral indígena* (Bogotá: Consejo Episcopal Latinoamericano, 1987) and José Alsina Franch, compiler, *Indianismo e indigenismo en América* (Madrid: Alianza Editorial/Quinto Cententario, 1990). See also: Bishop Julio Cabrera Ovalle, El Quiché, "Desafíos de la pastoral indígena en Guatemala," and Bishop Gerard Flores Reyes, "Una experiencia concreta: La Verapaz," *Misiones Extranjeras* 116 (March–April 1990): 122–29 and 152–56, respectively, and Giulio Girardi, *El*

derecho indígena a la autodeterminación política y religiosa (Quito: Ediciones Abya-Yala, 1997) and his *Los excluídos: Constituirán la nueva historia: El movimiento indígena, negro y popular* (Quito: Centro Cultural Afroecuatoriano, 1994).

14. Drawn from Brazil's Conselho Indigenista Misionario. See Juan Bottasso, ed., *Las misiones salesianas en un continente que se transforma* (Quito: Centro Regional Salesiano, 1982): 195.

15. See Series on Faith and Cultures: Contextualizing Gospel and Church published by Orbis and edited by Robert J. Schreiter.

16. Luis Jolicoeur, "Teología y culturas aymaras," *Teología y Vida* 36 (1995): 226.

17. See especially Stephen Judd, "The Indigenous Theology Movement in Latin America: Encounters of Memory, Resistance, and Hope at the Crossroads," in Cleary and Steigenga, eds., *Resurgent Voices:* 210–230.

18. See, for example, Michael Lowy, "Sources and Resources of Zapatism," *Monthly Review* 49, 10 (March 1998): 1–5.

19. Guillermo de la Peña, "Social and Cultural Policies toward Indigenous Peoples: Perspectives from Latin America," *Annual Review of Anthropology* 34 (2005): 717.

20. Physical copies of the text seem to have slipped into oblivion.

21. Charles R. Hale, "Cultural Politics of Identity in Latin America," *Annual Review of Anthropology* 26 (1997): 567–90. See also Francesca Polletta and James M. Jasper, "Collective Identity and Social Movements," *Annual Review of Sociology* 27 (2001): 283–305 and Judith A. Howard, "Social Psychology of Identities," *Annual Review of Sociology* 26 (2000): 367–93.

22. Despite some gains, indigenous provinces in Ecuador and Mexico lag behind non-indigenous provinces on indexes like the Child Rights Index.

23. Robert R. Barr, "Bolivia: Another Uncompleted Revolution," *Latin American Politics and Society* 47, 3 (2005): 69.

24. Kay B. Warren, *Indigenous Movements and Their Critics: Pan-Maya Activism in Guatemala* (Princeton, NJ: Princeton University Press, 1998).

25. Alison Brysk, *The Politics of Human Rights in Argentina: Protest, Change, and Democratization* (Stanford, CA: Stanford University Press, 1994).

26. She and her husband took a trip to Bolivia as a diversion from research in Argentina. See Brysk, *From Tribal Village:* ix.

27. Ibid. Brysk's earlier chapter was considered a seminal work on Indian rights as a transnational movement: "Acting Globally: Indian Rights and Information Politics in the Americas," in Van Cott, ed., *Indigenous Peoples:* 29–51.

28. John Peeler, "Social Justice and the New Indigenous Politics: An Analysis of Guatemala and the Central Andes," paper for Latin American Studies Association International Congress, 1998: 14.

29. In addition to references in other endnotes, see Xavier Albó, *Pueblos indios en la política* (La Paz: Plural Editores, 2002); Deborah Yashar, "Indigenous Protest and Democracy," in Jorge Domínguez and Abraham Lowenthal, eds., *Constructing Democratic Governance, Latin America and Caribbean* (Baltimore: Johns Hopkins University Press, 1996): 87–105; "Contesting Citizenship: Indigenous Movements and Democracy," *Comparative Politics*, 31, 1 (October 1998): 23–42; *Contesting Citizenship in Latin America: The Rise of Indigenous Movements and the Postliberal Challenge* (New York: Cambridge University Press, 2005); Christian Gros, *Políticas de la etnicidad: Identidad, estado y modernidad* (Bogotá: Instituto Colombiano de Antropología e Historia, 2000); Donna Van Cott, ed., *Indigenous Peoples and Democracy in Latin America* (New York: St. Martins, 1995); *From Movements to Parties* (New York: Cambridge University Press, 2005); Rachel Sieder, ed., *Multiculturalism in Latin America: Indigenous*

Rights, Diversity, and Democracy (New York: Palgrave Macmillan, 2002); David Mayberry-Lewis, ed., *The Politics of Ethnicity: Indigenous Peoples in Latin American States* (Cambridge, MA: Harvard University Press, 2002); Kay Warren and Jean Jackson, eds., *Indigenous Movements, Self-Representation, and the State in Latin America* (Austin, TX: University of Texas Press, 2002); Ronald Niezen, *The Origins of Indigenism: Human Rights and the Politics of Identity*; and Frank Salomon and Stuart B. Schwartz, eds., *The Cambridge History of the Native Peoples of The Americas*, vol. 3 *South America*, Part 2. (New York: Cambridge University Press, 1999). Ediciones Abya-Yala in Quito has published a number of volumes on indigenous and their movements.

30. James W. Wilkie, Carlos Alberto Contreras, Katherine Komisaruk, eds., *Statistical Abstract for Latin America* 31 (Los Angeles: UCLA Latin American Center Publications, 1995), table 3107: 990.

31. Kay Warren and Jean Jackson, "Introduction," in Warren and Jackson, *Indigenous Movements:* 1–46.

32. Anthony Stocks, "Too Much for Too Few: Problems of Indigenous Land Rights in Latin America," *Annual Review of Anthropology* 34 (2005): 85–104.

33. Ibid., 86.

34. Ibid., 86.

35. Donna Van Cott, *The Friendly Liquidation of the Past: The Politics of Diversity in Latin America* (Pittsburgh, PA: University of Pittsburgh Press, 2000).

36. See Van Cott, *The Friendly Liquidation*, table 4: 266–68 and Warren and Jackson, "Indigenous," *Annual Review:* 551.

5

The Landless

Each greedy individual preys on his native land like a malignant growth, absorbing field after field and enclosing thousands of acres with a single fence. Result: hundreds of farmers are evicted.

—Thomas More, *Utopia* (1516)

Each year when representatives of Christian base communities gathered in Brazil for their national meeting, they began their *encontro* by recalling the names of members who had been killed during the previous twelve months. When interviewed in 1989, Frances O'Gorman said that she and other participants in the encontro had placed 400 names of martyrs on the banner that stood each year in an honored place on the dais.[1] The most prominent was the name of Padre Josimo. Not only his name but also part of his bloody t-shirt was affixed to the banner.

Josimo became an iconic symbol not only of Christians involved in the fight for human rights but also of all persons, Christians and seculars, who threw themselves into what has become the Movement for the Landless (MST).[2] The Movimento dos Trabalhadores Rurais Sem Terra became the largest political movement in Brazil and one of the largest human rights mobilizations in the region, with many transnational partners. While the focus here is on Brazil, the issue of land has been contested in other countries, as well. The Movimiento Pro-Tierra, founded by Padre Andrés Girón, in Guatemala, and other movements have been created but none matches the sustained efforts of the MST and break-off groups in Brazil.

Padre Josimo Morais Tavares, one of the few Afro-Brazilian priests in the country, was killed on May 10, 1986, by Geraldo Rodrigues da Costa. The fact that his killer was identified was unusual since most murders were clandestine or became part of "public secrets," known but too dangerous to identify. Human rights proponents were heartened by the murderer's capture, trial, and imprisonment. Brazilian justice reverted to its usual practice of impunity in many similar cases. The names on the banner continue to multiply at every yearly encontro.

No other human rights movement has been as long-lasting and well-organized—and controversial—as the Landless Movement. The following sections take up, first, the historical background in which the issue of land arises. Second, the central section recounts the history of the Landless Movement, its somewhat unique organizational features, and entry into national politics. The final section takes up questions of globalization and framing of MST by the media.

LAND TENURE AS A HUMAN RIGHTS ISSUE

Land tenure waxed and waned in the 1960s–1980s in Latin America as a policy issue that affected socioeconomic development, not a human rights theme. After World War II, global attention shifted from rebuilding Germany and Japan to countries called the Third World. What became clear early in efforts to develop countries where agriculture was the main economic activity was that a major obstacle existed in the unequal possession and often unproductive use of land. Latin America had the world's largest reserves of arable land with an estimated 576 million hectares, equal to 30 percent of total territory.[3] Land reform was a special focus in the Alliance for Progress, the leading US effort at aiding Latin America in the 1960s.

What Che Guevara observed in the early 1950s, as depicted in "Motorcycle Diaries," was millions of peasants living in servitude to rich landowners. This servitude was the basis of many twentieth-century revolutions worldwide, including the Mexican (1918) and Bolivian (1952) revolutions. In Peru, where Guevara came face-to-face in the early 1950s with the landless, a progressive military government twenty years later saw land inequities as threatening national security. The military government expropriated large estates, including some of the most prominent. Generally speaking, though, efforts at land reform in Latin America were patchy and at best only moderately successful.

In contrast to many countries where land reform demands were met with indifference or hostility (as in Chiapas, Mexico), Brazil emerged as the one country where the issue has been most alive. The demand for change in Brazil was fueled by human rights concerns within a democratizing nation. This new impetus came in large part from believing in the rule of law. The new hope that something could be accomplished by action in the public sphere came from learning to resist military rule and repression using human rights motivations.

Brazil never had a significant land reform. The country has the second highest concentration of land ownership in the world. The exact percentages held by the top and bottom sectors are not known. A survey done in the early 2000s found that 90 percent of Brazil's private property was in the hands of 20 percent of the population while the lowest 40 percent owned about 1 percent, or, more sharply focused, the twenty largest landowners held more land between them than the 3.3 million smallest farmers. Further, two to four million rural families were landless. The numbers fluctuate because of short-term events such as droughts or displacements from land because of dam-building.

For the poor in rural areas, it was crucial to have land in order to earn a living and to provide for their families. Further, without land of their own on which to settle, the families had neither stability nor the ability to enroll children in schools. With few abilities other than rudimentary farming skills and with high employment, they were living in disastrous circumstances. At the same time Brazil's great land mass had some 350 million hectares of arable land. Vast areas of this land were unused. Some 150 million hectares were underutilized, including 20 million fertile and easily accessible hectares that could be farmed immediately, as stated by Brazil's National Institute for Settlement and Agrarian Reform (INCRA).[4]

The issue was not simply large-scale ownership of land, but the question addressed the effective-use principle: land rightfully belongs to a person who made it productive through his or her labor. Land ownership is justified by productive use and the claims to ownership of vast stretches of land not in productive use contradicts the views of secular and religious thinkers. This view has been the tradition of the Catholic Church and is a keystone of liberal secular theories, especially of John Locke. These philosophical arguments may add to understanding land rights, but fundamentally, Brazil took the most basic step by making effective land-use part of its Constitution. By contrast, many Brazilian landowners owned large tracts of land they had not seen, much less transformed through labor, as Angus Wright and Wendy Wolford have observed.[5] Further, as will be seen, many claims to land ownership were dubious or fraudulent.

The land-tenure patterns in Brazil were set centuries ago and, in contrast to Portugal, remained largely unmodified. The collapse of the feudal system in Portugal changed views of land rights in that country, as in most of Western Europe, but not in Brazil. To Portuguese rulers, at the time of conquest, it made sense to grant immense sections of land to subjects loyal to the throne. Portuguese holdings in colonial South America amounted to virtually a subcontinent. The crown had neither administrative manpower nor wealth to control its rural countryside. The crown therefore depended on landowners, as the overseers of large territories, to maintain peace and to provide a minimum of care for slaves and other farm workers.[6] This system continued with some modification for centuries.

Problems about land delineation existed from the beginnings of colonial rule. Land grants were written by Portuguese kings or their agents oftentimes without named boundaries. This was the beginning of a corrupt and violent system whereby grantholders preferred not to have determined boundaries; they would settle disputes by power in one form or another. Brazil has had a modest but talented pool of legal scholars and historians who have studied the history of land ownership in the country.[7] By and large, they agree that many large properties were acquired by means that ranged from dubious to clearly illegal.

One aspect of that illegality was a nefarious skilled trade that produced an abundance of false documents that purported to support land ownership. One of the techniques used to give paper an aged look was called *grilagem*. Crickets, *grilos*, were placed in a box of newly written false documents. The chewing action of the crickets, plus some additional weathering, gave the documents the look of antiquity and presumptive credibility. Grilagem expanded to mean any attempt to use fraud to acquire land. In 2001, the Brazilian government used the term grilagem to describe the extent of false claims. They found that at least 92 million hectares, an area 50 percent larger than the total land surface of Central America, had been claimed by fraudulent means. In one of its examples, the government reported that the state of Mato Grosso had issued more titles than there was land to support the titles. The report said that in the west of Bahia state, land ownership was being claimed for the same large property by four alleged owners, all with purported legal documents.

A more direct way to subvert the land title system, such as it was, was simply to set fire to the government land office where titles were registered. When this occurred in the southern part of Bahia state in 1912, a war broke out between old landowning families and new claimants. Again, a new vocabulary was developed: "burning the archive" also meant eliminating persons who had long and clear memories of who owned what. The keeper of collective memory was especially honored in a society highly dependent on oral history, and his or her elimination was equivalent to setting fire. Later "burning the archive" was extended to mean killing witnesses in court cases.

Finally, one of the most common ways to subvert the system was through manipulation of bureaucratic decisions about land boundaries. Given the predilection of large landowners not to have named boundaries for their land grants, this made it easier, with the help of corrupt bureaucrats, to encroach on public lands and the lands of others, especially smaller and less well-armed landowners.

Social status was deeply rooted in land ownership. This was especially true in the Portuguese colonial territory where universities were outlawed and secondary schools were few so that education as a pillar of status was weak or nonexistent. In a gross sense, the more land the greater the status of the landowning family. Further, since titles to land were often contested in unmapped territories and access to water and trade routes were of great importance, violence became a customary way to settle disputes. Common, too, was the practice of large landowners to control the officials who were to administer justice.

Thus, for human rights advocates to attempt to change customary land holdings or demand the administration of justice according to due process and the rule of law has been a monumental task, as the hundreds who have died in the process of trying to change these culturally embedded practices has shown. Just when progress in gaining public acceptance for land reform in 2005 was being made, the world media carried the news that Sister Dorothy Stang, an older American nun, was killed in the Amazon region for activism related to the reforms.

Paulo Freire and Modernizing Brazil

When Brazil emphasized modernization in the 1950s and 1960s, change of attitudes and values from traditional to modern in its citizens became a major theme. The country's leaders were obsessed with *grandeza*, with moving the nation toward greatness, exemplified in the building of a new capital city, Brasilia, immense dams, and the Transamazonic highway. Brazilian leaders were in what was called a Pharaonic phase. Planners saw the Brazilian peasant who formed a large part of the population as almost hopelessly fatalistic and illiterate.

Modernization demanded both an entrepreneurial attitude and literacy. The problem of "backward attitudes" was especially deeply rooted in the northeast. The northeast held one-third of Brazil's population at the time, with the lowest per capita income of Latin America and a very high percentages of illiterates. One of the main "change" projects of that era was the Movement for Basic Education (MEB). This movement began in 1961 by the Catholic Church with the cooperation of the government. Young Catholic Action activists formed part of the program's staff. A special target of this program was training adults to read and write. A notable shift was occurring worldwide from traditional schooling to the education of adults through informal education. In Northeast Brazil, Catholic Action activists became the creative force in making the MEB adult education program much more than traditional literacy training. A person considered to be one of the great educational innovators of the twentieth century, Paulo Freire, emerged as the organic intellectual of the movement. Most important for the discussion here, Freire contributed central ideas for Base Christian Communities, liberation theology, and a methodology for moving into action for obtaining one's human rights and those of others. He emphasized consciousness-raising, *concientição*. He was especially concerned with praxis: action leading to community improvement, action linked to values modified by trial and error.

In many ways, Freire created a philosophy that serves as the intellectual backbone of the landless movement. His ideas are now embedded in the patriarchical figures, as João Pedro Stédile, as well as in high school students and young adults in the movement. Central to virtually everything in the movement is the concept of a person as a subject who learns, a master of his or her own destiny, rather than being conceived as an object into which knowledge is poured. Freire offered a method of teaching and learning that is similar to John Dewey, Aquinas, and Aristotle in his emphasis on student-centered learning, but his pedagogy is more clearly radical. Learners are not objects to fit quiescently into a system but persons who understand society as it is and aim to make their own imprint on society to improve the system for themselves and others. In a word, Freire facilitated the shift in small farmers and rubber tappers taking part in these adult literacy campaigns from fatalism to empowerment, from accepting what life and the government gave to taking charge of one's own destiny, of reshaping one's social environment.

Further, Freire aimed at convincing peasants that they did have the power of agency, that they create their own culture through song, dance, demonstrations, marches, and Catholic and Lutheran liturgies. This often underdeveloped area of culture and creativity has found new fire in younger members of a movement now in its third decade, as will be noted.

The MEB was greatly diminished within a few short years when the military took power in 1964 and discouraged "change-minded" projects. Freire and some of his collaborators went into exile. However, his ideas, to be found in the *Pedagogy of the Oppressed*, became embedded in the lives of many Brazilians for whom justice and human rights became common cause.[8] Since first priority had to be given to working against military repression with imprisonment and torture, it was no surprise that a full range of economic rights was not emphasized in Brazil during the early part of the military dictatorship that lasted from 1964 to 1985.

Nonetheless, the first steps toward economic rights and what would become of the landless movement were taken in 1975 while the military was still in full control of the country and nongovernmental initiatives were frowned on. This first step was the creation of the Pastoral Land Commission, commonly called CPT, by the National Conference of Brazilian Bishops. Lutherans, who had been working among German immigrants, issued their own statement about land use. The churches, as the only institutions that were allowed a measure of freedom in the country, saw themselves as the voice of the voiceless. During the 1975 National Meeting of the Amazon Ministry, sponsored by the Brazilian Bishops Conference in Goiânia, participants focused on the drastic economic situation of persons who were farmworkers and other Brazilians attempting to eke out a living. The CPT was created to give spiritual care and to promote more just conditions for these people. The Catholic Church thereby provided an umbrella for persons caught up in an unjust situation made worse by military rule.

Scholars who have written histories of the MST point to its evolution from the CPT. In other important ways MST history is also bound up with the Amazon region. Madelaine Adriance in her widely-read *Promised Land: Base Christian Communities and the Struggle for the Amazon*[9] captured not only the conflicts faced, but also the faith-based community of the members of CPT. For the first time, many persons of peasant background within Christian base communities felt that by pulling together they would have the strength to change the society and culture in which they lived.

CREATION AND ORGANIZATION OF THE LANDLESS MOVEMENT

The CPT itself began among persons involved in the Catholic Church's pastoral efforts to Brazil's Indians through the church organization called CIMI. This Consehlo Indigentista Missionário (Indigenous Missionary Council) acts as the church's arm to offer pastoral and social care to the far-flung Indian tribes, including legal assistance to protect their rights.[10] While Indians in Brazil have received considerable global attention, they number less than 0.4 percent of the population. Church leaders felt that another specialized ministry was needed to deal with the land issue, one that affects a much larger population than the indigenous. Hence, the Pastoral Land Commission was created at the 1975 CIMI meeting.

Birth of MST

In early 1984, some one hundred landless and their advisers met at the diocesan hall in Cascavel in western Paraná. At an earlier meeting of CPT, José de Souza Martins, a CPT adviser who became a major figure in the landless movement, counseled the formation of a movement that would address the issue of land reform all over the country, especially the northeast where the need was especially great. The three-day meeting gave birth to MST, with João Pedro Stédile, originally an agronomist working for the Brazilian government, as its president. In many ways, the CPT prepared the ground for the MST. However, given substantial numbers of Lutherans and a sense of needing greater autonomy than being an organization tied to the Catholic Church, the founders of MST created an independent organization.

The next issue for the founding group was the relations of MST to rural farmworker unions. Since the landless felt their strength lay in involvement of the whole family—indeed, this is the hallmark of the movement—they decided to remain independent of the farmworker and trade union movements. The decision proved to be liberating for both women and for adolescents who found they possessed a voice in meetings and roles in the movement in ways dissimilar from the aforementioned movements. Further, MST founders decided against aligning themselves to political parties, even to Luis Inácio Lula da Silva's Workers Party (PT). Moreover, they defined themselves as not just landless, but the Movement of Landless Rural Workers.[11]

Stédile was especially well-fitted to be the long-term president of MST by his training as an economist and exposure to a wide range of opinions while studying at Mexico's giant National Autonomous University (UNAM) where he was influenced by Rodolfo Stavenhagen and other intellectuals.

The national political environment was changing as the military first "decompressed" and then prepared its strategy for exit from the Planalto presidential palace and for elections in 1985. Luis Inácio Lula da Silva and the unions carried on various industrial workers' strikes and demonstrations in the years leading up to the transfer of power from the military to civilians. In a word, this was the time of opportunity for the birth of a movement. A government is never as vulnerable as during a time of transition. Further, seeing that urban workers were demonstrating with lessened repression from the government, the rural leaders and advisers meeting at Cascavel were emboldened to push ahead with the landless movement. Clearly, the time had come for a national movement that would have greater political influence than the local or regional efforts. The landless had achieved a good deal in the southern states and now felt the need to spread to all sections of the country, especially the Amazon and the northeast.

To concentrate here briefly on the Amazon, the military government had attempted to put in place modernization plans for the region. These plans, drawn up without much regard for regional or local society, reinforced an already unjust situation. The plans also changed from time to time. Chaos followed. At one stage the government hoped to grant large tracts of land to mining interests in an area where few of the people on the land had clear title to what they thought had been their property, perhaps for generations. Many had no thought of land ownership, since they were basically no-madic tree-tappers or other workers who moved from place to place, fishing and hunt-ing in the vast wilderness. Encouraged by the military government, foreign and Brazilian investors had their eyes on vast tracts of land that could be forested for timber or burned over with the intent of using the land for ranching or agriculture. The latter proved an especially bad idea since there was barely enough topsoil to hold nutrients, or there was either too much or too little water, depending on the season. In the process, Brazilians left the world's largest rain forest frequently in flames and created the environmental and political nightmare described in *The Burning Season* and many other volumes.

Twenty years earlier, military preoccupations were made worse concerning the Amazon river basin because of an incipient guerrilla movement near the Araguaia River. Anticommunist fever led the military into a massive counterinsurgency cam-paign and repression over hundreds of kilometers in several states. It not only left the guerrillas dead before they fully organized, but it also pushed hopes for agrarian reform aside, as somehow catering to communists. (A number of rural leaders used a discourse similar to Marxists in condemning capitalism.)

Many investors from São Paulo and overseas became large landowners in the Amazon and elsewhere. This meant seeking rentier income and the need to protect in-vestment through gunmen and the use of violence to maintain order. These tactics had the tacit consent of the military for which security was of utmost concern. Jose de Souza Martins wrote: "Never in the history of Brazil did the *latifúndio* make such un-bridled use of private violence as during the military years."[12] Overall, from 1985 to 2000, 1,190 squatters, settlement members, farmworker union members, and human rights advocates were killed. Multiple banners mounted at yearly meetings are needed for all their names.

The problem of the landless became an issue in many parts of Brazil other than the Amazon. The building of new dams forced many peasants off their lands, but many more fell victim to the mechanization of agriculture in the fertile south, 1,500 miles from the Amazon region. Within a relatively short time, millions of Brazilian farm fam-ilies were landless. The Brazilian bishops, still in tension with the presiding military government, but acting as one of the few public voices the military could not control, took a bold step reported throughout Latin America by issuing a scathing statement, *The Church and the Problem of Land*.[13] The church noted that government land poli-cies favored the wealthy and deviated public monies to allow large companies to use it as their own. The bishops condemned violence by hired killers, sometimes in collusion with police.

Land Use and the Constitution

As the Brazilian military planned to leave the governing of the country in the mid-1980s, a great opportunity for reforms was offered activists, as noted elsewhere in this volume in the case of laws for street children. The government acceded to pressures and created an Agrarian Reform Law in 1985, and the constitutional assembly put forward provisions for land that were incorporated into the 1988 Constitution. Both provide that farmland that is not farmed productively can be declared "of social interest" and can be expropriated. In many ways, this provision is the foundation of human rights activity regarding land in Brazil and of the landless movement in the country.

What followed can be called "The Brazilian Way." This has two aspects. First, the legislators water-down laws. In this case, they modified some eight times the agrarian reform provisions. Second, Brazilians have grown accustomed since colonial times to the practice of making laws and then not enforcing them. In many ways, this is the heart of Brazil's democratic problem: will the laws be applied and thereby establish the rule of law as the norm? The expropriation law is seldom enforced, so land occupations are organized, and the government only acts because it has been pressured. To force agrarian reform authorities to expropriate and redistribute farmland, MST looks for sites that appear to be eligible for expropriation and then recruits and organizes the families that will be involved in occupations. Generally, several hundred families are involved. Some are found in the vicinity; others are recruited from some distance. They came together in their famous tent cities, with wide, black plastic sheets serving as tent covers. The next stage is political education and preparation for occupation and then settlement. In sum, MST organized large groups of landless farmworkers to occupy lands that are not being worked and then demanded expropriation.

This occupation can also be viewed as almost uniquely Brazilian. Above all, occupations are communitarian. Second, they involve families. Third, from the beginning, occupations have been rituals. One could view them as theatrical, as performance pieces that follow a well-understood script. (No wonder, then, that the landless movement translated easily into a hugely popular telenovela, as will be noted.) Lastly, they are dangerous. In 2003, the number of members killed during MST activities doubled from the previous year to 73 murders.

Settlements and Education

Through the years, the next phase, that of settlement on the land and its specific problems gained concentrated movement awareness. At the beginning, some settlers thought their problems would be solved once they occupied land. Not only are settlers sometimes faced with repeated attempts of previous landowners to intimidate them into leaving, but they have to struggle to fit into the patterns of globalized agriculture and to avoid environmental degradation. Through study and trial-and-error, the movement's agricultural efforts have proven themselves profitable enough to support settler families and to be environmentally sustainable.

In 1986, movement members discussed whether settlers should remain sem-terra movement participants when they were now com-terra. Most voted that they remain part of MST. The movement thus had to address new issues, including subsidized credit, grants to build houses and roads, and to have electricity and running water installed in the settlements. MST took steps to reduce haphazard occupation of land by families and arranged patterns that helped facilitate proximity of family residences and greater communication of goods and information. The manner of farming and sharing in profits as a community was a far more difficult question. By June 1990, MST chose as policy for its settlements a collective system of production. This proved to be a bad choice and resulted in a generalized fiasco. In reaction to the failure, some farmers turned to working individual plots. The general trend, though, especially after 1996, was to choose cooperatives as the route to the future. These cooperatives bought in bulk and set up marketing cooperatives, among many other functions. The Confedação Nacional das Cooperativas de Reforma Agraria do Brasil (CONCRAB) became the economic arm of the MST. It was built on trust, participatory decisions, and solidarity. Leaders of MST have expressed utopian goals for the settlements and for working within cooperatives. They have spoken of a new man and a new woman and the ultimate goal of reforming Brazilian society. While the description of these goals sounds hopelessly quixotic, it may help to recall that the well-accepted kibbutzim of Israel have similar goals. Kibbutzim exist as a minority within the state and grow slightly from year to year, numbering 117,200 persons in a national population of some seven million in 2005.

Living in the settlements has brought with it the same issues, such as marital infidelity and other problems, that marked life in the favelas or rural communities from which the settlers came. However, in contrast to the haphazard life of favelas, life in the settlement camps has a deliberate daily routine. Persons are placed in sectors, commissions, and other forms of organization. This brings people together, distributes power, and creates a strong experience of democracy. Everyone in the camp, young and old, has to take part in one of these groups. So, a young people's brigade keeps the camp clean. Health commission members deal with routine ailments. MST leaders believe that through these routines camp members learn to behave responsibly, despite life in the camp being a miserable experience at times.

The settlements also provided opportunities for the movement to create educational opportunities. To a certain extent, education is the main motivation for young families to belong to the movement. Angus Wright and Wendy Wolford have noted, "If the children receive a good education, then it is all worth it. If they do not, then everything else is overshadowed in failure."[14] MST leaders pursued a policy based on the principle that the arena of education properly belongs to government, so their target has been national, state, and municipal governments to provide financing for schools and for teacher training. They obtained help from Brazil's burgeoning universities for teacher training and found in the newer universities professors versed in Paulo Freire's methods that promote critical thinking as well as basic knowledge.

In general, the schools found in the settlements, say Wright and Wolford, are markedly better than comparable rural communities by quantitative and qualitative measures.[15] The movement created a national select high school in Veronópolis, Rio Grande do Sul. The school offers various programs of study for future farmers and leaders. The movement was reported to be running 1,200 schools in 2002, educating 150,000 children as well as 25,000 young people and adults in literacy courses.[16]

Following Freire's master ideas, schools emphasize both knowledge and values. The central value may be said to be participation. The planning, implementation, and evaluation of schools attempt to draw all stakeholders into these processes. The methods used, as interactive dialogue, are aimed at developing skills and knowledge by which landless children and adults will participate effectively in the movement and in society. To a considerable extent, the remarkable vitality of the movement can be attributed to its schools.

The Movement and National Politics

With membership of about 500,000 families and at least two million individuals by the mid-1990s, MST applied increased pressure for a more effective agrarian policy and practice. *Veja*, a major Brazilian news source, notes that there are at least twenty-seven autonomous organizations of rural workers, most of them inspired by MST but expressing other viewpoints. The Movement of the Liberation of the Landless (MLST) was formed in 1994 by militants on the extreme left, but as *Veja* says, in practice they do not differ much from the MST.[17] Despite diverse organizations, the main thrust of the sem-terra movement is carried by MST.

This movement offered the most unified and active opposition to so-called neoliberal policies of the popular two-term President Fernando Henrique Cardoso (1995–2003). "FHC," as he was commonly referred to, did respond to their pressures and redistributed significant amounts of farmlands. He was responding to pressures from MST, including grand public demonstrations. In 1997, for the first anniversary of the Eldorado massacre, the landless mounted an impressive thousand-kilometer march to Brasília, the national capital, from various parts of the country. This won wide support from the left. The next two years, 1998 and 1999, saw other national mobilizations in the March for Brazil and the March of the Excluded. These were followed by demonstrations opposed to genetically modified crops.

These magnificent public displays won public attention, to the extent that the newspaper *Zero Hora* wrote in an editorial: "There is no one with a minimal amount of information who does not support agrarian reform in this country."[18] While perhaps an exaggeration, the statement acknowledges attention gained by MST that once worked on the margins of national society. This impetus allowed MST to forge alliances and drew in university-educated, urban activists into staff positions, thereby adding a new level of political sophistication. Further, MST built links with some fifty Brazilian universities, adding a strong measure of respectability to what seemed to be a rag-tag confrontational army.

Thus, the issue of land reform emerged from the margin of national society's attention to become a central issue of national debate. Gabriel Ondetti has characterized this as a result of several factors, as the abrupt intensification of collective action for land reform after 1996 and other factors already noted. Ondetti argues that sparks for the abrupt intensification were the strong political impact of two massacres of landless members by official security forces at Corumbiara in August 1995 and Eldorado do Carajás in April 1996.[19] The author of this volume was resident in Brazil immediately after the Eldorado massacre and can attest to the national and international outrage expressed at the time that mobilized civil society organizations and focused national attention on the land issue.

MST and sister organizations increased land occupations in 1996 by about three times the amount of occupations in 1995. A clear case of repression that presumptively was intended to discourage protest served not only to engender more protest but also extracted more favorable response to the issue from the media and from the government. President Cardoso took several steps, including the creation of a new land reform agency in 1996. An unusually popular evening soap opera, "King of Cattle," based generally on the Eldorado event, was shown in 1996 and furthered contributed interest to the MST cause. However, this reaction was a short-term effect with the government. As memories of the massacres faded, Cardoso in his second term felt freer to cut spending for land reform, but by then MST had achieved greater acceptance as a political player on the national scene.

The next president, Luis Inácio Lula da Silva, also recognized the pressures of the MST. When he assumed the presidency in 2003, he said that land reform was a priority. However, it was far from clear that he had enough influence to push measures through the legislature, so MST mounted 1,700 protests that year. Lula did little. MST attempted to force the government to push through a decree to change the productivity index. This index was established in 1975 and was used to determine whether land is unproductive and thereby could be used to resettle families. Landowners lobbying congress strongly opposed the amplification of the decree. MST conducted a National March for Agrarian Reform in 2005 especially to pressure for reform of the productivity indexes and for settling MST families. MST stepped up its rhetoric through promising in March 2006 to promote a great wave of invasions.

The movement had become a major political player in Brazil but lacked effective linkage to legislative politics and faced the prospects of decades-long struggle. After suspending mass actions in 2002 at candidate Lula's request, so Lula would not be seen as sponsoring disruptive politics, MST was returning to the tried-and-tested method of mass direct actions.[20]

INFLUENCE OF GLOBALIZATION AND THE MEDIA

Small Farms in a Globalized Economy

A number of factors, including globalization, work against the Landless Movement. First and foremost, small farms, those of a few hectares, have little chance to succeed in a globalized world, unless dedicated to specialty crops. For development planning, economists pointed out that economies of scale meant that large farm holdings would be the norm in the future. For the United States, at one time, this meant that farms should probably be at least 800 acres in size if producing common commodities, such as corn. More resources than land were needed. Hundreds of thousands of dollars were needed for machinery and fertilizers. Just like other small capitalists, many Midwestern farmers took to reading the *Wall Street Journal*, with their eye on world markets. In California's Central Valley, 5,000 acres was barely enough to farm, given the need of employing large-scale irrigation systems.

The textbook case on globalization is South Africa where the small sugar-cane farm cannot compete well in the export market against (ironically) the giant sugar plantations of Brazil. However, no economist at the University of Chicago or at a large state agricultural school interviewed by the author advocated a sudden disappearance of all small farms. There would have to be a period of initial adjustment from small-scale farming and some provision of a safety net. Moreover, small holdings, at a minimum, were a way to survive. One could at least eat what one grew and barter for other necessities, as peasants have done since peasantry appeared in the world.

Some of the ideology by landless leaders put forth in the early days of the movement stressed the need for small landowning as the foundation of nation-building. That rationale has been toned down or lost, as Brazil's agribusiness achieved recognition as a great commodities resource for the world and has been courted by China to supply that country's immense need.

Whether MST farmers, now or in the future, will be part of this bright future is debatable. It is far from clear that MST has provided a viable economic alternative to agribusiness. Zander Navarro, a sociologist at Rio Grande do Sul, believes that neither MST nor its settlements will prove efficient enough to survive. He wrote: "The settlements as a general rule will provide no more than a temporary afterlife to families that lost their plots of land earlier and gained a reprieve in the settlements."[21] Others have argued that in California, France, and Italy, small farmers have found a sufficient living through organic and specialty farming and may serve society far better than some of the poisonous and wasteful methods of industrial farming.[22] The Amish and the Mennonites may show a way to survive. For the time being, Brazilian MST settlers have the freedom and the right to try to succeed. The alternative of being a poorly-paid fieldworker, ingesting pesticides and being subject to the ups and downs of world market prices is far less attractive.

A second factor has been a notable shift away from rural problems to urban ones. Brazil's population has gone in a relatively short period from being 75 percent rural to being 75 percent urban where effective political activity is centered.

Another factor has been the shift toward liquid assets, as Brazilians become increasingly entrepreneurial within the world's eighth largest economy. This shift renders fixed agricultural property less important. This shift occurred in the 1946–1964 period when a larger share of wealth was to be found in land. Those holding liquid assets could move them by exiting the country when dangers are perceived as when presidential candidate Lula da Silva was seen as a radical socialist in 2002. Many entrepreneurs were thought to be ready to exit the country. Land, of course, cannot be moved and is under threat of expropriation, taxation, or onerous regulations. Landowners, thus, especially need their clientalistic ties to power and rely on police, military intervention, and hired gunhands to protect their holdings that are seen as no longer the main sources of power and prestige.

Land as a contentious issue has notably declined in Brazil. Despite the sensationalist news stories of Brazil's being courted by China for its commodities, drawing Brazil away from the United States, agriculture amounts to only 10 percent of Brazil's GDP. Urbanization and industrialization reduced the socioeconomic and political importance of the agricultural sector. Kurt Weyland and others have noted that the highly unequal distribution of land as a contentious issue once contributed to the downfall of the weak democracy that existed in the early 1960s and led to military takeover.[23] Anthony Pereira described the end of Brazilian peasantry as occurring by the late 1980s.[24] In the early 1960s, Brazilians considered land reform as the second or third most important problem in the country. By 2000, they did not consider agrarian reform as even one of the fifteen most important national problems.

Landowners, thus, had less support for their violence as purportedly necessary to prevent an explosive revolution. Landowners also saw widespread rejection of their reactionary UDR party (Democratic Rural Union). Popular support or tolerance of the Landless Movement is a more complex issue to be taken up at another point. At the same time, one should note that the possible threat of the landless undermining democracy is not the major preoccupation of many Brazilians as it once was. This also makes it easier for the churches and others to focus on the landless as a human problem, not primarily a political one.

The Movement and the Media

In one of the first historiographies of the MST, Cliff Welch described the "alarmed criticism" of "nearly every news vehicle in the country" about association with the MST.[25] John Hammond said that most Brazilian scholars offering analysis of media coverage of the MST described that coverage as "unequivocally hostile."[26] The Brazilian scholars see in this coverage an alliance of big landowners and big capital, of which major media are a part. Hammond himself went to considerable effort to analyze systematically how the media has portrayed Brazil's largest sociopolitical movement. He presents a more nuanced picture than Welch. (Portrayal of the movement in major media in the United States, it should be noted, has been fairly even-handed.)

The relationship of media and movement matters a great deal. The media play a crucial role in both public and government acceptance of the movement and in shaping the issues surrounding the movement. At the beginning, the movement leaders cultivated a spirit of independence. They kept a degree of isolation from the press and, as noted, consciously separated themselves from churches, trade unions, and political parties. However, as the organization evolved from its modest inception, MST leaders made special efforts since the early 1990s not only to get media attention but to help frame the issues as portrayed by the media.

Contrary to Brazilian scholars, Hammond found that Brazilian media coverage has been diverse. He used a standard methodology of media research, employing various frames of analysis for analyzing content. Ultimately, Hammond concluded that print media was often favorable to MST as an organization. However the press did not necessarily encourage the goal of mobilization that the movement sought to promote.

Televised fiction was different story. A highly unusual source, a telenovela featuring the landless, made a splashy appearance. In contrast to day and evening soap operas in the United States, Brazilian telenovelas often have a defined beginning and conclusion, seldom lasting more than a few months or a year. The telenovela "O Rei de Gado" (The King of Cattle) ran for several months on a major network, O Globo, in 1996–1997. This occurred not long after the landmark massacre of landless demonstrators at Eldorado de Carajás. The telenovela was one of the most popular of recent years and portrayed the unnamed but easily recognizable landless organization in a favorable light. That telenovelas reach beyond those who read newspapers was gratifying to movement supporters.

The massacre at Eldorado de Carajás stands as one of those landmark events captured almost by accident on video and broadcast and rebroadcast on television as Brazilians watched in a way similar to North Americans watching the beating of Rodney King in Los Angeles. In 1996, 2,000 MST farmworkers blocked a highway to demand that the government expropriate an almost 6,000 hectare ranch. In full daylight and without provocation, the uniformed police fired on the demonstrators, killing nineteen and wounding others. A television crew caught in the traffic jam on the highway filmed part of the massacre. They did not catch the full field of action, as forensic pathologists later attested that at least ten of the protesters were executed at extremely close range. Protests in reaction to the killings took place all over Brazil, including an ecumenical service at São Paulo's Catholic Cathedral. Despite the notoriety of the event, only the two commanding officers were convicted six years later. (It was unlikely that the police acted on their own authority.)

Movement leaders also fostered their own publications for internal communication and external good will. They are well aware of citizens' media and provide educational materials for schools and maintain low-power radio stations in communities created on occupied farms. They maintain a first-rate website in Brazil and through their friends' websites in other countries and languages. Cellphone use and the internet allowed leaders to communicate with participants in remote areas during crucial times of negotiations about land occupations.

The movement is much better anchored with institutions in Brazil and globally than it was in 1984, its foundation year. MST works with not only the Pastoral Land Commission but many other activist groups, including the Confederation of Agricultural Workers and the National Housing Movement; public administrators in various ministries; UNESCO and UNICEF; religious relief agencies, such as CAFOD; and more than fifty universities in Brazil and elsewhere.

Cultural Representations and the Future

The MST has been fortunate in receiving attention from performing artists and a notable photographer. In general, during the period of military dictatorship, singers such as Cayetano Veloso and others in Brazil called attention to the plight of the poor, especially the landless poor, through coded messages whose contents were clear to most listeners. After the dictatorship, Chico Buarque has returned from time-to-time in his songs to dramatize the plight of the landless.[27]

A world-class photographer, Sebastão Salgado, portrayed the lives of members of MST in barren surroundings, but conveying persistence.[28] His *Terra: The Struggle of the Landless* contained master works in black and white. Salgado's pictures were featured in exhibitions in New York City and European cultural centers, increasing foreign awareness of the landless cause. Salgado's images win critical accolades, especially in France where he resides, but the images further ingrained ideas of a tattered, joyless, amateur movement. This movement has changed, and Salgado could now use color to depict joyful celebrations and liaison meetings of movement leaders and university consultants.

Within Brazil, even the style of the MST marches has been choreographed to a degree that draws mostly favorable attention, especially from Brazilians who admire style in all they do, as in soccer. MST uses color, such as bright red scarves and pageantry, with banners to increase visibility for the movement.[29]

As a Brazilian journalist has noted, the face of the MST has grown markedly younger.[30] Younger members have absorbed the spirit of Paulo Freire who argued thirty years previously that peasants do create culture, high and low, and should create culture that carries attitudes and values that contest mainstream values. One of the main cultural vehicles has been grassroots theatrical productions. These productions have been notable features mounted by the MST Youth Collective during the National March for Agrarian Reform and other large events. The young people have taken their productions to regional events in Venezuela and Guatemala.

CONCLUSION

To the surprise of many observers, the Movement of Landless Rural Workers has not only persevered but also grown in numbers of members and in accomplishments. They have survived murderous opposition, faced hardball world economic forces, and suffered severe failures and internal conflict, in addition to the daily woes of heat, hunger, and discomfort. However, they managed to settle more than 350,000 landless families on what had been unproductive land. They have won significant public support[31] and have maintained a high level of mobilization for twenty years, unusual among very large social movements. The Foreign Policy Association calls the Landless Workers Movement one of the most successful grassroots movements in the world.[32]

The movement bears watching not only because of its size and success but because of its engendering a culture that promotes creativity and sharing, even while survival of members was being threatened by hired gunmen and corrupt police. Indeed, more than a thousand members and their advocates, including a priest and a nun were murdered. The movement and its members may yet be defeated by market forces of a globalized economy, but for the near future they will be content, as one of them said, to advance from one small victory to another. Further, they are impelled by some inner conviction to make the journey not as individuals but in solidarity with others. In the Latin American tradition of human rights, the journey is typically not a lonely one.

NOTES

1. Interview, Notre Dame, IN. March 19, 1989.
2. An abundance of works has grown during the history of the landless movement. Cliff Welch provides a useful overview of key works on the MST in his "Movement Histories: A Preliminary Historiography of the Brazil's Landless Labor Movement," *Latin American Research Review* 41, 1 (2006): 198–210. To his list should be added, Anne-Laure Cadji, "The Landless Rural Workers' Movement in Contemporary Brazil: Social Movement or Political Organization?" Ph.D. diss., University of Oxford, 2004.

3. International Research Institute for Climate and Society website, viewed June 27, 2006.

4. Ana Maria Galano, "Land-Hungry in Brazil," *Unesco Courier* (1998), posted at unesco.org, June 19, 2006.

5. Angus Wright and Wendy Wolford, *To Inherit the Earth: The Landless Movement and the Struggle for a New Brazil* (Oakland, CA: Food First Books, 2003): 23.

6. Gilberto Freyre described the plantation society in his *A Casa-Grande & Senzala*, a book that revolutionized the studies of Brazilian history.

7. See, for example, Paulo Guilherme de Almeida, *Aspectos Jurídicos da Reforma Agraria no Brasil* (São Paulo: Hucitec, 1990); Fabio Alves, *Direito Agraria Fundiara no Brasil* (Belo Horizonte, Editora del Rey, 1995); and Paulo Tommin, *Institutos Básicos do Direito Agrario* (São Paulo: Saraiva, 1991).

8. Paulo Freire, *Pedagogy of the Oppressed* (Englewood Cliffs, NJ: Prentice-Hall, 1972). Virtually every academic library in the United States purchased the book.

9. Madeleine Adriance, *Promised Land: Base Christian Communities and the Struggle for the Amazon* (Albany, NY: State University of New York Press, 1995).

10. For an account of the growing activism of CIMI in defense of the indigenous, see Sue Branford and Oriel Glock, *The Last Frontier: Fighting Over Land in the Amazon* (London: Zed, 1985): 193–203.

11. For other types of people who work the land and Portuguese names for them, see Sue Branford and Jan Rocha, *Cutting the Wire: The Story of the Landless Movement in Brazil* (London: Latin American Bureau, 2002): 24.

12. Jose de Souza Martins, *O Poder do Atraso: Ensaios de Sociologia da História Lenta* (São Paulo, Editora Hucitec, 1999): 83.

13. An English version is contained in Edward L. Cleary, ed., *The Path from Puebla* (Washington, DC: National Conference of Catholic Bishops, 1989): 349–57.

14. Wright and Wolford, *To Inherit:* 254.

15. Wright and Wolford, *To Inherit:* 254–55.

16. Paulo Gentili and Tristan McCowan, *Reinventar a escola publica: Politica educacional para um novo Brasil* (Petropolis: Editora Vozes, 2003): 2.

17. *Veja On-Line* (March 23, 2006).

18. Quoted in Crista Berger, *Campos em confronto: a terra e o texto* (Porto Alegre: Editora da Universidade, 1988): 170.

19. Gabriel Ondetti, "Repression, Opportunity, and Protest: Explaining the Takeoff of Brazil's Landless Movement," *Latin American Politics and Society* 48, 2 (2006): 61–94.

20. James Petras and Henry Veltmeyer, *Social Movements and the State: Argentina, Brazil, Bolivia, Ecuador* (Ann Arbor, MI: Pluto Press, 2005): 111–13.

21. Quoted by Bradford and Rocha, *Cutting:* 238–39.

22. For a discussion of small farmers, see, for example, Wright and Wolford, *To Inherit:* 279–87 and Branford and Rocha, *Cutting the Wire:* 264–84.

23. Kurt Weyland, "The Growing Sustainability of Brazil's Low-Quality Democracy" in Frances Hagopian and Scott Mainwaring, eds., *The Third Wave of Democratization: Advances and Setbacks* (New York: Cambridge University Press, 2005): 102.

24. Anthony W. Pereira, *The End of Peasantry: The Rural Labor Movement in Northeast Brazil, 1961–1988* (Pittsburgh, PA: University of Pittsburgh Press, 1997).

25. Welch, "Movement Histories": 199.

26. John Hammond, "The MST and the Media: Competing Images of the Brazilian Landless Farmworkers Movement," *Latin American Politics and Society* 46, 4 (2006): 62.

27. See website: landless-voices.org maintained by the University of Nottingham.

28. Sebastão Salgado, *Terra: The Struggle of the Landless* (London: Phaidon Press, 1998).

29. George Yudice, "Afro Reggae: Parlaying Culture into Social Justice," *Social Text* 19, 4 (2001): 62–63.

30. Christiane Gomes, "Brazil's Landless Youth Come of Age," *NACLA Report on the Americas:* 52.

31. Hammond, "The MST and the Media": 83.

32. Website posting at fpa.org, June 15, 2006.

6

Policing

To dial the police is to ask for a beating.
—Brazilian slumdweller

Military or authoritarian governance in the last third of the twentieth century brought policing forward as a human rights priority. This became a special focus as police were employed to enforce order in authoritarian regimes then typical of Latin America. Their heavy-handed practices continued in fledgling democracies. Further, a dramatic increase in crime in the 1990s brought increased attention to ineffectual policing. Governments, political parties, and nongovernmental groups have all moved toward improving the human rights involved in providing public security.

Americans, though, may be at a considerable disadvantage in understanding either the sense of insecurity or the lack of respect for police that Latin Americans feel. Using the question about whether one feels safe walking in the dark, 82 percent of US respondents agreed that they felt safe, higher than citizens of most other developed countries surveyed.[1] (By contrast, only 70 percent of persons in the United Kingdom felt safe walking in the dark.) Presumably this sense of security is much greater than most Latin Americans, whose fear of crime is commonplace.

Then, too, North Americans stand at the top of the list of citizens of seventeen developed countries for their trust in police efficiency. This may come as a surprise, given all the attention to police-local tensions that periodically appear on newscasts. Eighty-nine percent of persons in the United States said they believe that police do a good job controlling crime in their area.[2] Surveys showed only 16 percent of Argentines and 33 percent of Brazilians expressing confidence in police.[3]

The following sections take up, first, what police do that causes concern for human rights advocates. The section also recounts the history of policing that has embedded police in corrupt practices. The second section addresses the fundamental relations of policing to democracy and special Latin American issues, such as the historical ties of police and military, women's issues, and imprisonment. The third section describes and analyzes the mobilizations taking place to address policing and human rights and some measures, effectual and ineffectual, to reform policing.

CONDITION OF LATIN AMERICAN POLICING

When a frequent visitor to Latin America goes through an intersection as the yellow light begins to appear and a police car stops the person, panic ensues. Does the policeman expect a bribe? The first thing for the driver to remember is what country one is in. Suborning a policeman is not an expected practice in Chile or Costa Rica or, perhaps, Uruguay.

That policing practices differ among Latin American countries can be seen clearly in the US State Department of Human Rights reports on individual countries under the heading of "Respect for the Integrity of the Person, Including Lawful Freedoms." Here one may gain a sense of how police of various countries treat citizens concerning basic human rights. Where a democratic tradition has been well established, as in the three countries named above, police do not use excessive force as a general practice. However, in many other Latin American countries, police are an organization to be feared or avoided, not trusted. As a Brazilian favela dweller said: "People here fear the police and their guns more than they do the [drug] dealers."[4]

The general condition of policing in many countries could be described as having episodic killings and brutality by police and prison officials. Supervision of policing is often inadequate. Impunity and corruption remain serious problems. Overcrowding and substandard conditions in jails and prisons continue. These problems are compounded by inordinate delays in investigations and trials.

To use Bolivia, a country praised for its democratizing efforts,[5] as an example, the Adenauer Foundation showed that 30 percent of all complaints made to the Public Defender were about police abuse of human rights. Further, in Bolivian opinion polls, the police were thought to be among the most corrupt institutions and as having low credibility. Similar or worse reports have been made about police in a number of other countries. In Ecuador, security forces committed unlawful killings. The police beat or otherwise abused suspects, detainees, and prisoners. Persons were subject to arbitrary arrest and over 70 percent of detainees in jail had not been formally sentenced.

In Central America, extrajudicial killings by security forces were common before the 1996 Central American Peace Accords. They remain a problem in Honduras. Now the issue of policing is compounded by the use of private security forces. Increasingly, security is being privatized in Central America and elsewhere, but private forces, unlike the ones seen in Europe or the United States that patrol gated communities, also act as death squads. Organized private and vigilante security forces in Honduras were believed to have committed a number of extrajudicial killings, particularly of young persons.

One complaint about police that is commonly heard in countries like Peru is harassment. After instances in which police have used unjustifiable force or severely injured detainees, victims and the families are harassed to keep them from filing charges, further weakening confidence in police and making police reform difficult.

The inefficiencies of policing, coupled with local government corruption, have led to people taking matters in their own hands. This has taken several disturbing forms. In some slums, such as Brazilian favelas, drug dealers provide a measure of security and a predictable code of conduct. In Colombia, private armies control large areas of the country, or, more spontaneously, vigilante justice takes over. Diane Davis is only one of many to observe the "emergence of vigilante mentality."[6] The Brazilian favelas spawned a special beast among vigilante types, the *justiceiro*. These self-appointed enforcers or just freelance killers were shown in a notable segment of *Sixty Minutes*. One justiceiro shown on the CBS program, Corporal Bruno, achieved mythical status, with national notoriety.[7]

Justiceiros lasted some decades and are declining now, for reasons that will be explained. Brazil's favelas were akin to the Wild West due to precarious forms of territorial occupation (no clear land titles), absence of government, and inferior local organizations. As in thirteenth-century England or eighteenth-century United States, men had almost complete freedom to attempt to impose their wills, with little fear of legal judgment. Justiceiros served a function of imposing some order, protection, and retribution for victims of crime who wished that perpetrators be punished or eliminated. Political will, civic consciousness, and drug cartels brought an end to or a severe decline of the reign of justiceiros in the São Paulo region by the late 1990s.

Traditional Justice

Some of what appears to extralegal killing is customary or traditional justice. Indigenous communities have had their own justice systems from time immemorial. These systems were tacitly recognized by the Iberian rulers in colonial times and by national governments since that time. Governments have taken steps toward their formal recognition as an integral part of the national justice systems.

Traditional, not constitutional, justice rules in many remote areas of Latin America. It is only now receiving academic attention.[8] What outside observers seldom appreciate is the short reach of the regularly organized police force and, for that matter, the reach of governmental control in general, in several countries. It used to be said in the 1960s that the Bolivian, Peruvian, Guatemalan, and Mexican governments only controlled society within fifty miles of large and mid-sized cities. After that distance, local strongmen were in control and traditional justice was carried out. Bolivia was one of the first countries to recognize local or regional government by indigenous after the 1952 National Revolution. Decision making by indigenous *caciques* and other officials was recognized by the national government and institutionalized through a specially created and powerful Ministry of Indigenous Affairs and Agrarian Reform. Thereafter, formal authority was recognized as being invested in local authorities, including life-and-death decisions.

The nearest parallel in the United States may be Jim Chee and the other characters involved in southwest tribal justice system, as depicted in Tony Hillerman's mystery novels. The contrast between what Hillerman portrays of the United States and what takes place in marginal areas of Latin America is very wide. Lynching by Indians and other rural dwellers is still carried out. Dozens of alleged criminals and corrupt mayors have been burnt alive or hanged in the twenty-first century. What takes place in remote areas came to world attention when American and European travelers were threatened with death by Guatemalan indigenous communities. Community members believed the rumors that they had heard that Guatemalan babies were being snatched by foreigners. Clearly, the observance of human rights by agents of traditional justice is a major issue still needing attention.[9]

Other Issues

Another problem of policing that troubles human rights activists is crowd control. In several countries, for example Peru and Bolivia, police and military have handled crowds poorly—with lethal force and lethal effect. This has been going on for decades. However, Bolivians no longer accept lethal force as a routine and acceptable manner of keeping order. In 2004, Bolivians did two previously unthinkable things. First, they held a once-popular president, Gonzalo Sánchez de Lozada, accountable for the deaths of numerous persons by the military attempting to control demonstrations, forcing Sánchez to flee the country. Second, they were not satisfied, as they would have been in the 1960s with his resignation; they demanded repatriation, a juridical process, and possible long punishment for Sanchez. Impunity does not reign unchallenged.

Lastly, police in some areas, such as Mexico, are so bad that they seem unreformable. When a new police chief was named to clean up Nuevo Laredo in 2005, he was dead within a day. Nonetheless, national governments, Mexico's included, have made good-faith efforts for some years to reform the police, as will be noted.

History of Policing

The explanation for the corrupt condition of much of Latin American policing can be found, in large part, in the history of the policing institution in the region. In brief, the security forces from the newly independent republics (1810–1826) that evolved into contemporary police forces were expected primarily to keep public order, not solve crimes. From the beginning they were poorly paid, ill-trained, and treated as part of the servant class. Indeed, they were virtually servants of the privileged and powerful. If a policeman in Brazil caught a person of the privileged classes in a minor offense, the standard response to a police challenge was: "Do you know who you are talking to?"

Both the police and the military were key elements in the formation of the independent Latin American states that were formed after separation from Iberian rule. For a long time after the 1810–1826 Independence War period, most countries had contested histories with civil wars, contests between Liberals and Conservatives, rivalries among caudillos, attempted revolutions, and—to this day—conflicts between regions of a country. Bolivia, with its 190 regimes in 145 years, is an extreme example of contested governance. Administrations came and went. The police and the military continued on as the supporting pillars of the state and public order, like a family watchdog, faithful but underfed.

One aspect that is striking about Latin American police history is resemblance to the police of the United States in the periods of industrialization. The fact that industrialization was state-led in Latin America as contrasted to the laissez-faire type in the United States only increased the ties of Latin American police to state power.

During industrialization, an active and politicized working class and a large service sector emerged in Latin America, often among European immigrants, primarily in cities. Many persons in the working classes were imbued with Socialist ideologies. Governments counted on police to keep working-class leaders and unionists in line. They did this mounted on horseback in the best European tradition and apparently with some relish, judging from the historical photographs from Argentina, Brazil, and Mexico of mounted police swooping down on crowds of striking workers. Much of union organizing took place in secret. Shopkeepers also organized clandestinely to respond to or to demand state regulations in order to control chaotic buying and selling practices. The police needed ground-level intelligence of what was being planned in secret by workers and shopkeepers, so that the state and its close allies, the economic elite members, could continue to monitor them. Thus, the state and industrialists used police not only to dominate workers but also to control the inevitable political parties that were created to represent worker and shopkeeper interests. The use of police as agents of intelligence for control by elites has many negative implications for democracy.

Legitimate opposition to government or economic elites was sometimes viewed in itself as subversion. Hence, freedom of the press has a rocky history in Latin America, in part because of police informers. The classic case of misuse of national intelligence has been that of the Peruvian intelligence chief Vladimiro Montecinos, who in the 1990s collected all sorts of intelligence on political and other leaders. This intelligence was used for bribery and for the financing of presidential political campaigns.

Police intelligence work and what Diane Davis calls the street-level capacity of police to make or break shopkeepers and other service-sector folk increased the status of police officials from servants of the economic and political elites to virtual partners in power. The teeming masses of the nineteenth-century cities needed government regulations seemingly for everything from the just calibration of store scales to minimal fire walls and the disposal of waste. The police were charged with enforcement. Opportunities for bribery and other corruption were abundant.

Besides their diverse relationships to industrialists, the working class, and the service-sector in towns and cities, police in rural areas typically served the best interests of landowners and received favors in return. In rural or remote jungle areas, this police protection of landowner, logger, or petroleum company interests may be somewhat diminished but generally continues unchecked since colonial times. If not actively assaulting rural workers, as at the Eldorado de Carajás massacre in Brazil in 1996, then security forces seldom investigate and almost never succeed in convictions of landowners or their agents suspected of homicide, physical intimidation, or threat (also a crime). Brazilian police activity forms a major part of the context of the Landless Movement's struggle, as detailed in another chapter in this volume. Guatemalan security-force complicity with the rich or powerful fills the file cabinets of groups like the Guatemalan Human Rights Commission.

Money passed along to police and military by shopkeepers or by industrialists and landowners for regular and special duty saved the state from increasing salaries. It also kept the state's security forces relatively content. Decades of developing this kind of cronyism and cozy arrangements with wealth and power might take just as long to reform.

In sum, police were more interested in control than solving crime, more interested in serving special interests, their own included, than protection of ordinary citizens. It is no accident that there have been few iconic Latin American policemen in Latin American literature.[10] Fiction is based on verisimilitude and the idea of detectives solving crimes is more a joke than a nearly true story.[11]

As Latin America's law system, based on the Napoleonic Code, differs from that of the United States, so, too, does its policing system. In a number of countries, two types of police function. One organization patrols, enforces, and turns over suspects to the second group; the other investigates and may move the state toward legal processing of criminals. In Brazil, the first police force is called Military Police when, in fact, they are not under military jurisdiction. The second has been given the name Civil Police. In Chile, the first type are the *Carabineros* (similar to the Italian *Carabineri*); the second are named *Investigaciones*.

The two types of police forces named are dispersed under control of the separate Brazilian states, or, in some countries, they may be national in scope, as in Chile. Further, some municipalities also have their own forces. Often there are traffic police or treasury police. Coordination between police forces is generally poor and often competitive. In a word, organizational structures hinder crime prevention, help explain the growing crime rates despite sizable police forces, and foster corruption by lacking clear lines of accountability.

Police are certainly not lacking in numbers in some countries. Colombia has the 12th largest police force in the world; Chile, a relatively small country, has the 24th largest force. Transposed to per capita figures, Colombia ranks 31st and Chile 38th worldwide. As noted, Latin Americans have greatly supplemented police protection with private security forces. Libertarians may rejoice at this outsourcing, but social justice advocates feel that the poor and vulnerable are often unprotected except by drug cartels and community vigilantes.

POLICING, DEMOCRACY, AND SPECIAL ISSUES

The United States in its annual human rights reports on other countries places policing high in its considerations of human rights. This emphasis can also be found in the two major transnational human rights organizations, Amnesty International and Human Rights Watch, both with European origins. Does this emphasis on proper police conduct signify a North Atlantic cultural difference from Latin America, or, perhaps, the emphasis indicates that developing nations are at any earlier stage in political development when policing is still on its way to higher professional standards?

In Latin America, human rights organizations were slow to address rights violations by police in the South and Central American regions.[12] In the great tide of human rights organizing that began under military governments in the 1970s, the police were considered to be a secondary problem. As noted in other chapters, there were more urgent targets: stopping death and disappearance at the hands of military or authoritarian regimes that took place in all but a handful of countries. Further, police generally kept the middle and upper classes—the classes that mattered to politicians—secure and maintained public order. How the security forces did that, many felt, was better left unexamined.

However, regard for and observance of the rule of law is fundamental to society and especially to democracy. If those charged with maintaining the rule of law do not offer vigilance, or worse, abuse the rule of law themselves, democracy and human rights do not have an opportunity to flourish. The international thrust toward democracy and the rule of law, known as the Third Wave of Democratization of the 1970s,[13] made clear to Latin Americans that their policing did not measure up to the minimum standards of democratic behavior. Their European and American economic trading partners found police abuses unacceptable and applied pressure for reform.

It is difficult to talk about anything other than a shell democracy when arbitrary detention, torture, and ill treatment and misuse of the judicial system are common, as Amnesty International says of Mexico in its 2005 report.[14] Human Rights Watch states that several of Mexico's human rights problems stem from shortcomings in its criminal justice system. They include torture or other ill treatment by its law enforcement officials and a failure to investigate those responsible for human rights violations.

Great pressures for reform were felt by Mexico from the United States and Canada in the late 1980s and early 1990s when Mexico wished to enter into the North American Free Trade Agreement. Both trading partners insisted that Mexico make institutional reforms leading to improved observance of human rights. Mexico's key policymakers (the outgoing President Raul Salinas and incoming President Ernesto Zedillo) at the time, with Ph.D.s from Harvard and Yale, respectively, both understood well why Canada and the United States were so insistent on the rule of law.

While Latin Americans had been fatalistic about changing the habits of the police, now, as Diane Davis notes in a recent essay: "across Latin America, political parties and government officials are identifying public insecurity and unrule of law as among their greatest challenges and police and judicial reforms as important goals."[15]

Crime and Democracy in Latin America

Crime did not become a grave issue in the region until relatively recently. Visitors to Latin America in the 1960s and 1970s loved the night life in Latin America that went on until the early hours of the morning without danger, as long as one stayed away from the worst sections of cities. Buenos Aires was considered the safest capital in the developing world, even in the 1990s. Now, crime is at the head of the list of concerns for many citizens.

There is not a single cause for this increase. High unemployment has driven some to criminal paths. Conspicuous consumption by economic elite members set up attractive targets for criminals. A plentiful supply of guns and people who know how to use them, especially deriving from the civil wars of Central America, have contributed to crime and violence. Probably the greatest increase in crime has been due to drug production and transportation. Beyond growing and trading drugs, Latin Americans are now themselves bitten by drug addiction. They did not fall into drug use in ways that were typical of Europeans or North Americans for the first decade or so of the contemporary cocaine trade in the 1970s, but now many Latin Americans are addicted to drugs. Crimes related to drug use followed in ever-increasing volume. Such mountains of money went into crime cartels that analysts worried that Mexico and Colombia were becoming narco-states.

Violent crime has become a grave personal problem in many Latin American countries. Polls show that very high percentages of citizens say that they or someone close to them has been a victim of crime. A study done by the Inter-American Development Bank calls the levels of victimization "staggering."[16] In this study, six countries, including Mexico, showed more than 40 percent of urban households had at least one member victimized during the previous year. (Researchers presumed that most of the crimes were property crimes.) In seventeen countries surveyed, the rates of victimization ran from 25 to 55 percent.

As fear of crime climbed considerably in the last twenty years, an explosion has taken place in private security forces, walls with razor wire, and gated communities. Internationally, some Latin American countries have become notorious for violence. Colombia and El Salvador stand at the top of the list worldwide for their homicide rates. Colombia, Mexico, and Brazil topped the world for kidnappings.

As awareness of crime grows, so has the private security business. In Brazil, the Federal Police registered some 4,000 firms that employ 540,000 employees who attempt to provide private security services.[17] These figures do not include an uncounted host of unlicensed providers. (The informal and unlicensed economy, in general, is huge—maybe half the size of the formal economy—in Latin America.) Private security forces are especially notable in Central America where they provide a measure of assurance for foreign visitors and *la gente decente*. However, the backgrounds of private guards are often shadowy. Further, reliance on private outsourcing hardly makes up for poor organization and implementation of strategy in the public sector. Sooner or later, governments have to provide or supervise trained and regulated forces for the protection of their citizens, even if some security protection is outsourced.

Thus, a profound issue about democracy has arisen in some Latin American countries: the more they democratize, the more crime enters their life. For them, the correlation between democracy and crime seems strongly positive. Authoritarian governments appear to some Latin Americans better at providing safety. Hence, many Latin Americans are ambivalent about their new democracies. The question arises: could rising crime rates push Latin Americans away from democracy and foster retrograde desires for military governments or authoritarian figures, for example, allowing Hugo Chávez to increase his authoritarian control of Venezuela?

Military and Police

Police frequently became intertwined with the military in attempting to maintain public security. For the last one hundred years, the Latin American military rarely has been called upon to fight another country. The last major war ended in 1933. The military has been assigned what many assume is a valuable role for them: the assuring of internal security. This role helps justify their existence, whereas Costa Rica did away with its armed forces more than fifty years ago, saving lots of money for education and health, areas in which Costa Rica excels. In other countries, militaries break up strikes, protect the incumbent president, and, in general, help to keep public order. They have been the ultimate inner shield for Bolivia's presidents and have been used from time-to-time to control or confront the police in that country, mostly recently in 2003.

Military men, many of them have told the author, do not like to do "police" work.[18] They regard this as being unprofessional. In fact, the Latin American military does police work poorly. They do not have good local intelligence; their armaments tend to be broad and indiscriminate killing machines; and they have a culture in Latin America as being apart from civilian life. Hence, some military leaders have been eager to defer to the police for surveillance, making arrests, and imprisoning dissidents and troublemakers.

The relations of military and police that existed from the times of independence became much more intermingled during the period of military governments from the 1960s and into the late 1980s in some countries. Police and military were combined under unified commands. At one extreme, their conduct ranged from being agents of the states that killed, tortured, or generally terrorized the populace through intimidation and threat, as in Argentina, Uruguay, Chile, and Guatemala, or they became more focused on control of the public square. They did this through emphasis on intimidation and intelligence gathering about political parties, union leaders, and community activists, including priests and nuns. Much of this repressive policing was done in a Cold War atmosphere in the name of the doctrine of national security.[19]

When Latin American nations turned to democracy, authoritarian policing practices remained as a legacy.[20] Not only repressive, even punitive, policing measures remained, but also some police forces still served as branches of the armed forces, such as Chile's Carabineros. Further, military courts continued to process essentially civil cases. Issues arising from civil liberties violations by police both served as a drag on an already undemocratic institution and as a trigger for looking at policing in a new light and doing something about it. "Few changes measure the deepening of democratic standards better than the control of state security forces that have long been instruments of repression and have acted with impunity," as Pereira and Unger have noted.[21] Reforms of these authoritarian tendencies will be discussed later.[22]

What should be noted here are two current trends in some, but not all, countries. While militaries generally were pulling back from police work in the new democracies, the drug war has pulled the military back into policing. Not only were they attacking the sources of production or processing, as in the Andean countries and Mexico, but also raiding Brazilian slums controlled by drug cartels. The Brazilian military attempted to wrest control from drug cartels on several occasions. So, too, increase of common street crime, apart from direct relations to the drug trade, made assignment of the military as street patrols a measure of last resort.

The police themselves have become militarized. Some units look and act like military: helmets, vests, boots, and faces in gothic black. Police policy, too, drifts towards military solutions rather than neighborly, persuasive, preventive activity. This trend, as practiced in the United States, has had articulate opponents from the right and left wing of public opinion. As far as can be determined, little active opposition to the militarization of the police exists in Latin America where civil liberties are fragile entities and perhaps such trends are easily overlooked.

Women and Policing

Women are receiving special attention in relation to police work. Latin Americans have been leading the way toward contributing a gender perspective to the issue of security. Adding much larger numbers of women police officers and making provision for their promotion to higher ranks has been long overdue and is being accomplished through most of Latin America. One reason for their inclusion in police forces was to modify the masculinist culture that has dominated Latin American policing.

Similar changes toward inclusion of women are occurring in many world regions. However, Brazil has taken the lead in creating an innovation: women's police stations. Brazilians have argued that female victims of crime often require special services due to rape and domestic violence and a need for privacy and discretion. The first women's police station (WPS) was created in São Paulo in 1985. Primarily women police officers staff these stations that focus on crimes against women. The number of women's police stations quickly rose to 125 in São Paulo state and 339 throughout Brazil.[23] Seven other Latin American countries have followed Brazil's example,[24] as have countries in other regions.

Brazilian women activists made their proposal for WPSs as the military was leaving the government after twenty-one years of rule and as special police stations were being set up for Afro-Brazilians and for the elderly.[25] Women activists argued for the same model. José Gregori, Brazilian Secretary of State for Human Rights, believed that the specialized police stations helped to address the inequalities expressed in violence against women and were the consequence of the large number of women who were active for human rights in terms of death and disappearance in the 1970s and 1980s.[26] For most of Brazil's history violence against women was not considered a crime. By the mid-1980s women activists were able to extract from the state recognition that violence against women, including domestic abuse, was a crime.

Typical WPSs are small and unadorned. The chief officer is called *delegada* and the staff includes four specially trained officers to register the women's complaints, five detectives to investigate, and three trained psychologists for counseling. A television, a coffee machine, and a children's playroom are available.

The gender perspective contributes to democratic policing. Women's police stations increase awareness of women's rights, especially among the lower social classes. The stations provide greater access to justice for the disenfranchised; they reduce the geographical and psychological distances between where the poor live and where help is available. The collaboration between women's grassroots nongovernmental organizations, government agencies, and police have helped to spin a tighter web of civic society and democratic governance. Then, too, a gender-specific approach to policing is consistent with more democratic, service-oriented policing, beyond authoritarian order-maintenance.

The women's stations have, however, what the Vera Institute of Justice and others characterize as serious limitations. The stations are found in only 10 percent of Brazilian cities. The hours when the stations are open are limited to daytime, while many instances of spousal or other abuse occur in the evening. The number of prosecutions for sexual abuse seems not to have increased. Some female officers resent working in specialized stations rather than being assigned to "real" crimes with greater opportunity for advancement. Moreover, female officers are not necessarily more gender-sensitive than their male counterparts.

Through interviews, Cecília Santos investigated the important questions about the effectiveness of WPSs, the issues of being "special," and the relationships of female officers and feminists. Santos found that some policewomen made explicit alliances with feminists. Another group of policewomen wanted no contact with feminists and preferred working on "real" crimes. A third group—and one that has become predominant after 2001—embraced aspects of feminist discourse on violence but did not make explicit alliances with feminists. Thus, the relations between policewomen and feminists have been changing, as views of some policewomen have shifted in their opinions over time.

Overall, one may say that women's police stations are consistent with the trend toward democratic policing and help to move the issue of domestic violence from the private to the public realm. The stations probably represent a transitional stage toward a wider recognition within society and its police forces of the abuse of women as "real" crime. The stations may be replaced by other approaches in the future.

Imprisonment

Policing and jailing became inextricably linked in the minds of many Latin Americans during the time of authoritarian rule in the 1970s and 1980s. A person stopped by police for questioning or for minor offenses in the United States does not automatically expect to go to jail, but being stopped by police on the street or in one's car in Latin America became an ominous occasion. Being picked up for questioning meant going to jail and entry into an abyss. In the 1970s, so large a number of citizens were picked up that large public spaces—stadiums, such as the national stadium in Santiago; military schools, such as the Naval Mechanics School in Buenos Aires; private mansions, such as Casa Grimaldi in Santiago; and storefronts, such as an auto agency in Buenos Aires—had to be used to accommodate the detained. What happened in these venues became legendary, achieving mythical status in books or enshrined as monuments to hellish experiences of torture and death on the spot or of being thrown out of airplanes into the ocean.[27]

One of the telling statistics came from Uruguay. One of every fifty Uruguayans went to jail in the 1973–1985 period. Uruguay was considered one of the strongest democracies in Latin America. Uruguay had been frequently described as the Switzerland of Latin America. Hence, its citizens were shocked at the large number of neighbors and relatives who were sent off to jail. This, indeed, was the intended effect of the police and the government: to shock the populace into fear as a way to control a small group of guerillas, or as a general threat that opposition to the government was not tolerated.

Those picked up were often from middle-class backgrounds. No one seemed immune. Even former generals were questioned and jailed for long periods; some former generals died at the hands of torturers. To a great extent, the middle classes became acquainted with a justice system that turned on them and not just on the lower and criminal classes. Some of the impetus for considering the connections of policing, jailing, and human rights comes from this Latin American experience since much of the energy and creativity for human rights protection derived from the middle levels of society.

A further step toward securing control was taken in Uruguay and elsewhere: torture of detainees became systematic. Typically, torture was prolonged and intense. For many detainees, the experience was seared in their minds and recurred over a period of many years as a form of post-stress syndrome.

The mental images of being picked up arbitrarily and of being tortured without due process remain for older Latin Americans and have been passed on by word of mouth to younger ones. This discourse of fear of police and of the need for recognition of rights had more or less free play to continue within families and in society. It also had reinforcement in notable Latin American films.[28]

One of the least "developed" aspects of Latin American society and of human rights advocacy is its prison system. While notable advances have been made in dealing with some gender issues and weighty attempts have been made at improving the judiciary,[29] prisons remain as ugly blotches on the landscape. From country to country, Latin American prison officials communicate only infrequently with one another for sharing reform policies or any other reason. Records barely exist, and country statistics do not compare well because ministries of justice have yet to explain what their records mean. In terms of human rights, this is truly a "Black Hole."

However, a comparative perspective needs to be kept in mind. The size of the Latin American prison population is nothing like that of the United States. The United States leads the world with 715 prisoners per 100,000 persons of the general population. Latin America's two largest countries, Brazil and Mexico, have less than one-fourth the prisoners per capita percentage of the United States. Both countries have 169 prisoners per 100,000 persons in the general population. Three Andean countries are in the 59–102 prisoners per 100,000 general population range. Ecuador's prisons held 7,716 persons, far below a comparable cohort in the United States.

Small steps have been made in prison reform. Uruguay's Socialist government, headed by Tabaré Vásquez, made human rights crisis in prisons a top priority. The legislature and the administration invited the transnational group the Association for the Prevention of Torture and a representative of the Inter-American Institute of Human Rights to come to Montevideo in April 2005 to discuss the creation of several legal and practical torture prevention measures that included appointment of a prison ombudsman with ties to human rights groups in the country. Further measures are described in the chapter on torture.

If Latin Americans have left the prison issue largely unaddressed, then one may presume that human rights advocates of the region have their attention focused on other issues or, more likely, that there has been no trigger, no structure of opportunity for moving governments to reform. Two possible triggers have not sparked reform efforts. First, Latin America stands out from other regions of the world in the high percentage of pretrial prisoners. This clear injustice—65–90 percent unsentenced in some countries—should have moved governments to act, but the situation remains uncorrected. Second, from time to time, prisons have exploded in flames caused by prisoner riots and a heavy-handed response, notably in Brazil, Peru, and Venezuela. Dozens, even hundreds, of prisoners have been killed in these riots, often with pictures of fires and waves of armed responders displayed on television sets. The riotous prisons' names, such as Lurigancho (Peru) or Caradiru (Brazil), are as familiar as Attica prison used to be in the United States.

Reasons for overlooking the conditions of prisons alleged by outside observers include Latin America having one of the highest violence indexes in the world. The threat of violence at almost every turn in, say, São Paulo, permeates the body and soul. The fear of violence and crime can foster a disregard for human rights and diminish one's views of citizenship, as Teresa Caldeira has so well depicted.[30] Perhaps more important for ignoring human rights issues in prisons is the predominant ideal of citizen security, that of living in an environment of peaceful coexistence with others. Increased criminality, public alarm, media alarmism, and distorted assertions have led to a view of keeping the peace by locking up troublemakers. Capture of criminals, harsher sentences, and more police personnel seem like the best responses. Increasing prison populations and disregarding prison conditions go hand-in-hand with the belief in the preeminent human right of ordinary citizens to a measure of security provided by the state.

Worse than the lack of recognition that prisoners, as human beings, have some basic rights, many Brazilians began to be opposed to human rights. Brazilian opinion-makers—politicians, talk show hosts—and many middle-class persons came to believe that human rights were "privileges for bandits." This was a change from the days under military dictatorship in the 1970s when human rights groups were cheered on in their efforts to protect political prisoners. After the release of political prisoners as the military eased out of power, prisoners who were crowded in jails were common criminals and the ones believed to be responsible for the climate of violence. In the 1980s, prisoners were pictured as being less than fully human. Then democracy, which was new to Brazilians, was blamed for excessive permissiveness and license. Indeed, as previously noted, democracy and an increase in crime were correlated. Further, in a world of limited resources, politicians argued that money would be better spent on schools and hospitals than prisons.

This opposition to human rights began to change in the 1990s with the election of Fernando Henrique Cardoso as president and Mário Covas as governor of the key state of São Paulo. Both tried to curb human rights violations. Cardoso succeeded in passing a National Plan for Human Rights with a strong cabinet-level Minister of Human Rights José Gregori. Human rights received favorable attention in mass media. Prisoners, and the general public, seem ignorant of their rights and lack legal assistance.

The Brazilian Catholic Church, for one, spent a year in the late 1990s attempting to educate Brazilians in the justice issues related to imprisonment in the country. The Church also acted as mediator in prison conflicts and has taken special pains to portray both the unjust conditions under which prisoners often live and the innate rights prisoners have by being human beings (and children of God). Churches, in fact, seem to be the only organizations regularly in contact with prisoners.[31] Nuns have been especially courageous presences in prisons like Lurigancho.

Nuns have also led the way in making outside human contact available to women prisoners. Latin American countries have been among the top countries in the world for female prisoners; they comprise seven of the top twenty countries in percentage of women prisoners. This ranges from Bolivia's almost 18 percent of women in the prison population to Guatemala's almost 7 percent. Since so little is known about the characteristics of prison populations, one can only speculate that a number of women were captured while acting as couriers for the drug trade, an occupation shown in the widely circulated film, *María, Full of Grace*. Women entering prisons, most of which were designed to hold men, have experienced special indignities, especially in coed prisons.

From the early 1980s until the mid-1990s imprisonment rates increased, mostly in the range of 23–76 percent. Not only were more persons being jailed, but they stayed longer, although not because some judge sentenced them. Being prisoners without sentence has become the norm, not the exception, and this status can last ten years. In some cases, untried or unsentenced prisoners have been confined without trial or sentence for twenty years.

The consequence of this situation is inhumane overcrowding. Some prisons are "ticking bombs." [32] Bolivia has an overcrowd factor of 162 percent, where overcrowding of more than 120 percent is considered critical. The ticking bomb may also explode because of the shortage of prison guards.

Increased international attention to the prison problem was focused through the Human Rights Watch's Prison Project, Amnesty International, Washington Office on Latin America, the United Nations, the Wilson Center, the Ford Foundation's Prisons in Crisis Project.[33] All these groups were friendly allies trying to tell Latin Americans disposed towards human rights protection that something important was missing in their efforts toward establishing justice and democracy. Domestically, some attention to the issues came especially through newspapers[34] and the Catholic Church. From the mid-1990s, governments attempted reforms. However, these were partial steps that were inadequate or that faltered because of chaotic judicial processes or poor policy creation or administration. These are similar to police reforms that will be described below.

One Brazilian prisoner expressed probably what many others are feeling: "We committed a crime and are paying our debt to society, but no one deserves to live like this, like animals." Amnesty sums up what they found: "Prisoners are packed into dark, airless, vermin-infested cells. They are exposed to life-threatening diseases and live in constant fear of assault by other prisoners or torture by prison guards or police."[35] Leaving prisoners in hellish conditions where health, life, and conscience are assaulted remains the major void in a Latin America that has advanced farther in human rights protection than most developing regions. As many have noted, prisoners forfeit their liberty, not their rights. Latin Americans may be practicing a dangerous form of moral exclusion: placing prisoners outside of one's moral concerns because of their presumed guilt and therefore their forfeiture of rights. This is a dangerous frame of mind in a democracy because the right to physical integrity and other rights do not depend on innocence or guilt.[36]

MOBILIZING FOR HUMAN RIGHTS AND POLICE REFORMS

In the author's view, it is essential for democratic functioning that groups organize for demanding and obtaining better policing, since it is unlikely that governments alone will do so. Newly-formed or well-established nongovernmental organizations demanding greater public safety became more common in the late 1990s. Often these organizing efforts have been tied to promises by newly-elected political parties that advocated police reform and/or abatement of crime as part of their electoral campaigns. Neighborhood groups, now part of the civil society fabric following the Mexico City earthquake or military government's economic debacles elsewhere, pushed for neighborhood security as they previously did for provision of water or electricity.

A dramatic taking to the streets in organized demonstrations to demand reforms occurred in 2004. Hundreds of thousands of citizens gathered three times in Buenos Aires and once in Mexico City to protest personal insecurity and crime and to demand police reforms. As the *Economist* noted, this was a long overdue but incipient push from civil society for reform.[37]

One of the potential venues for reform is the neighborhood. However, neighborhood groups have limited, spotty effect, in part because in face-to-face meetings with police, many ordinary folk are intimidated by badges, notepads, and uniforms. Larger, citywide groups may have more impact. Davis has called attention to INCESI in Mexico City, an organization funded by the private sector.[38] INCESI developed a massive public relations campaign about police corruption. The group also named in their organization's publications police officials known to be involved in illegal activities. They have managed this audacious activity in a relatively repressive society through funding and reputations of wealthier elite members of the group.

Also crucial for response from the private sector have been foundations. This was in contrast to the United States where foundations, often embodied in the form of think tanks, are common actors in public life. The kind of philanthropy that establishes centers, institutes, and museums for the public good was as uncommon in Latin America as it has been in Spain and Portugal. That is changing in Latin America where one now finds a mix of North Atlantic and Latin American foundations. Some, such as the Brazilian Braudel, Banco Real-Arno, and Vargas Foundations and the US-based Tinker, Rockefeller, and Ford Foundations have been crucial in thinking about and supporting efforts to reshape policing and security. They provide institutional backbone and a measure of what one might call comparative wisdom, a transnational view. Further, modern (as contrasted to traditional) universities are also offering intellectual leadership.

Brazil's premier Universidade de São Paulo (USP) sponsors an exceptional program, the Center for the Study of Violence, with ties to many regions, including Africa.[39]

Even institutes whose main concentration has been on the economy focus on crime and policing, for good reason: violence carries a heavy economic price tag. The Getúlio Vargas Foundation estimated that in 2002 the private and public sectors of Brazil spent US $37 billion on security, and not all of it was well spent.

Brazilians have made progress in crime reduction in some areas through mobilization by citizens and by state and local governments. Diadema, a municipality between São Paulo and São Bernardo with 376,000 inhabitants, had extremely high homicide rates. In the late 1990s, the rate was running at 141 per 100,000 population, the highest in São Paulo state and among the highest in the world. By 2003, the rate declined by half to 74 per 100,000 and was declining even further through 2004.

Many factors entered into the decline. A turning point occurred in 1997 when amateur videotape of the police torturing and killing presumptive young criminals was shown on "O Globo TV" network. In 2000, the Fernand Braudel Institute acted as a catalyst for civic mobilization for police reform and for diminishing the killing.[40] The institute began four years of work in the municipality by organizing a Public Security Forum that met monthly in the City Council chambers with local police chiefs, and civic, political, and religious leaders. New policies emerged from the meetings and slowly produced results, due to political will and the development of public institutions and the maturing of civil society.

This successful effort did not start from a level of primitive fatalism among the inhabitants. Older residents of the municipality had valuable experience in organizing themselves against the military government and for workers' interests in the 1970s. The Partido de Trabalhores, the Workers Party, which carried Lula to the presidency in 2003 and 2006 had a relatively strong presence in the city. The residents brought their experience of activism to the monthly meetings sponsored by the Braudel Institute. From these meetings many initiatives followed, including paving and widening streets to allow for better police patrolling, better lighting, and economic measures that encouraged a large expansion of small stores and the support of consumer credit to stimulate local commerce. The two branches of Brazilian police—patrol/enforcement and investigative—placed larger numbers of police and more trustworthy officers in the city. The success in reducing crime in Diadema was not isolated and stands as one example in the reduction in violent deaths taking place in Greater São Paulo. In sum, one of the major, but not only, reasons for the decline was the various measures to reform policing.

On a larger scale, within the state of São Paulo, a state wherein 35 percent of national Gross Domestic Product is generated, business leaders acted with a sense of crisis about the crime situation and joined with Globo Television and the Center for the Study of Violence to sponsor an international conference on crime in Brazil in May 1997. The conference was planned long before the televised police brutality in March 1997, but the televised events increased a sense of urgency.

The conference spawned a major new initiative, the São Paulo Institute against Violence (ISPCV). The main business associations joined in this effort to play an active role in police reform. This effort moved beyond the traditional efforts at strengthening their own private security. The effort made economic sense since the Inter-American Development Bank estimated that Brazil lost more than 10 percent of its GDP due to the costs violence inflicted.

ISPCV, as an independent agency, was charged with developing innovative policies, programs, and actions. One of its suggested programs, Crime Stoppers, was created in 2000. By August 2004, the program had received 270,000 calls about crime and criminals and led police to solving 9,000 crimes. ISPCV coordinated the establishment of human rights observatories in which youth groups were trained to collect and analyze information and produce reports on human rights in their communities. They also identified human rights violations and best practices to protect and promote human rights. This led to a national network of human rights observatories in 2003. These were but a few of the innovations proposed and adopted. In sum, one of the most promising sources of police reform has been the private business community. The new public-private partnership was clear evidence of a move away from authoritarian policing.

Police Reform

Apart from Brazil, plans to reform policing in Latin America have mostly disappointed expectations. Proposals for reform have been abundant. Many of them are add-ons, superficial correctives, or partial cures that sometimes make the situation worse.[41] Argentina moved toward reform through purges of police and of military intelligence; it changed the criminal code, created civilian boards, improved judicial oversight, and modified police training. Still, notable problems remain, including low accountability.[42] One proposal, not infrequently heard from economists, is to pay security forces more so they will not be tempted to depend on various forms of corruption for additional income. The result in one place was to make corrupt police even richer.

Again, one has to question whether states and their governments can reform policing without strong mobilization of human rights and civic organizations. Latin American states would not have accomplished much for women's rights without women's organizations, as seen in chapter 2 of this volume.

Political parties increasingly took up police reform in the 1990s and have intensified their efforts as crime increased. New presidents at the beginning of the twenty-first century—Norberto Kirchner, Hugo Chávez, Vicente Fox, and Lula—vowed that they would address police reform and reduction of crime. This policy initiative, as noted, is driven by strong and growing public sentiment. Even if this generation of politicos fails, the next generation will probably have an anticrime, pro-police-reform mandate.

Mark Unger has argued that so far police reform tends to embed the police closer within the state where they are affected by budget cuts and more closely bound to a weak judiciary. In the cases of Argentina and Venezuela, countries Unger examined, embedding the police more closely in the state led to further abuses of power.[43]

Can Rudy Giuliani, New York's former mayor, reform Mexico City's cops? With a consultant's fee of a million bucks or so? So ran the headlines in both cities. New York police did achieve a notable, and more importantly, long-lasting drop in crime rates. Analysts said the NYC reduction was due to changes in policing and in the environment (picking up abandoned vehicles), though no one knows for sure since many of the potential perps were in prison by the time Giuliani went from prosecutor to mayor.

Crime and its reduction have achieved worldwide attention. Police administrators and think tanks in Brazil now survey the world for visions and methods that work.[44] Latin America is very much in the flow of globalized information. Drawing from global research and from the experience of former Brazilian police officials turned researchers, the Braudel Institute in 2003 proposed policy recommendations. At the top of the list was reduction in homicides, especially in areas where the homicide rate is above 40 per 100,000. Since Brazil was a world leader in homicide by gunfire with about 40,000 gun homicides yearly, or about 88 percent of all homicides being caused by small arms, gun control became a key political issue. To its credit, given the heavy drag of Brazil's fragmented politics, the government brought the issue to a national vote in 2005, one of the few countries to do so. Brazilian voters defeated the proposal, but widespread attention to the issue was generated. Various publicity measures were used. In Rio, a central lagoon was topped by 40,000 white crosses floating on its surface to call attention to the large number of gun deaths at the time of the national vote.

The other targeted area for reform by Braudel was reducing police corruption that included improved systems of control and vigilance. Given the great organizational fragmentation of law enforcement, far greater cooperation between national, state, and local police officers was called for. Since Brazil has in place a national secretariat for public security (SENASP), the hopes of the Braudel people was that a cabinet-level post for public security would create greater policy attention and action.

All these and other proposals made by Braudel and others may seem like illusory dreams to outside observers. The proposals resemble proposals for reform made in Chile and Mexico. About those in Mexico, Diane Davis believes that only wide changes in the environment will bring truly effective changes, and these will be achieved over a long time. The alternative to not trying to change is worsening disorder, the kind faced by failing states, for example, Colombia, Guatemala, Haiti, and several African nations.

CONCLUSION

What one may say with certainty is that the reduction in crime in Diadema and other areas of greater São Paulo stands as an achievement of what can be done with police, politicos, and civic leadership, even in the short term.

Further, Latin Americans have clearly stated for themselves the close relationship between policing, human rights, the rule of law, and democracy, in contrast to traditional, fatalistic views citizens had of the men and women in police uniforms. As Paolo Freire is rumored to have said, the step of an ordinary person in Brazil away from fatalism is a greater achievement than the step of a US astronaut onto the moon.

What can be stated at the end of the first decade of the twenty-first century is that Latin American governments have worked hard and with some discernible success to increase public security through better policing.[45] In contrast to this perception, most polls and media coverage show that the general public believes little progress has been made to improve public security and that police-reform efforts have not reduced the causes of police brutality and ineffectiveness. As Bailey and Dammert report, the record is one of relative success.[46]

Human rights groups working on police reform have taken root in the region. Their presence strengthens democratic policing and enhances a changed view from the previous era in which human rights organizations came into existence. Policing and justice administration in the twenty-first century is substantially different from that under military and authoritarian governments. This is true not only in urban areas where policing receives the most attention but in remote areas where indigenous groups have acquired the concepts and tools needed to confront abusive state officials.

NOTES

1. United Nations International Crime Victims' Survey displayed at nationmaster.com.

2. UN International Crime Victims' Survey displayed at nationmaster.com.

3. The relationship between democracy and trust is well established in political science literature but the question of trust in police is typically ignored.

4. *New York Times* — Gun control story, October 24, 2005.

5. Bolivia was counted as one of five consolidated democracies in Latin America at the beginning of the twenty-first century.

6. Diane Davis, "From Democracy to Rule of Law," *Harvard Review of Latin America* (Fall 2002), online.

7. "Getting Away with Murder," segment of CBS News, *Sixty Minutes*, December 1, 1991.

8. Rachel Sieder, "Recognizing Indigenous Law and Politics of State Formation in Mesoamerica," in Sieder, ed., *Multiculturalism in Latin America* (New York: Palgrave Macmillan, 2002): xx.

9. A promising program for policing in remote areas, Policía Comunitaria, has been created in Mexico. See Allison W. Rowland, "Local Responses to Public Insecurity in Mexico," in Bailey and Dammert, eds., *Public Security:* 187–204.

10. Inspector Espinosa created by Brazilian writer Luiz Alberto Garcia-Roza is a notable exception.

11. This may be changing. Argentine writers are leading the way in the production and criticism of the police novel. The First International Congress on the Police Novel was held in Cordoba in 2005. Also, as Amelia Simpson notes in her *New Tales of Mystery and Crime from Latin*

America (Cranbury, NJ: Associated University Presses, 1992): 13: "The search for truth and justice [by the Latin American detective] frequently fails."

12. Melissa Ziegler and Rachel Nield, *From Peace to Governance: Police Reform and the International Community* (Washington, DC: Washington Office on Latin America, 2002).

13. Samuel Huntington, *The Third Wave* (Norman, OK: University of Oklahoma Press, 1991): 76.

14. Human Rights Watch 2005 Annual Report, section on Mexico: 1, online, March 2006.

15. Diane Davis, "From Democracy to Rule of Law."

16. Alejandro Gaviria and Carmen Pagés, "Patterns of Crime Victimization in Latin America," Working Paper #408, Inter-American Development Bank, Oct. 29, 1999: 6.

17. Staff report, "Public Security in Brazil," *Braudel Papers*, No. 33 (2003): 3.

18. Interviews in Brazil, Bolivia, and Argentina, 1967–1982 and among foreign student officers at the Naval War College, 1995–2000.

19. Edward L. Cleary, *Crisis and Change* (Maryknoll, NY: Orbis Books, 1985): 146–66.

20. See the pioneering efforts of Manuel Antonio Garretón on these legacies and the more recent work contained in Katherine Hite and Paola Cesarini, eds., *Authoritarian Legacies and Democracy in Latin America and Southern Europe* (Notre Dame, IN: University of Notre Dame Press, 1994).

21. Anthony Pereira and Mark Unger, "The Persistence of the Mano Dura: Authoritarian Legacies and Policing in Brazil and the Southern Cone," in Cesarini and Hite, eds., *Authoritarian Legacies:* 264.

22. It is exceedingly difficult to determine what police practices are more due to the traditional authoritarian state's history and what was determined more by association with the military in the late twentieth century.

23. Cecília MacDowell Santos, "Engendering the Police: Women's Police Stations and Feminism in São Paulo," *Latin American Research Review* 39, 3 (October 2004): 30.

24. The International Centre for the Prevention of Crime lists Argentina, Colombia, Costa Rica, Ecuador, Nicaragua, Peru, and Uruguay.

25. Andrew Downie, "A Police Station of Their Own," *Christian Science Monitor* (July 20, 2005).

26. Response to audience question at University of California by José Gregori, Berkeley, May 3, 1999.

27. See Horacio Verbitsky, *The Flight: Confessions of a Dirty Warrior* (New York: New Press, 1996).

28. Among many films, *The Official Story* and *The Night of the Pencils* stand out.

29. See esp. the Ford Foundation's efforts to improve the judiciary in the Southern Cone countries.

30. Teresa P. R. Caldeira, *City of Walls: Crime, Segregation, and Citizenship in São Paulo* (Berkeley: University of California Press, 2000): esp. 339–75.

31. Chile's Catholic Church helped establish the Confraternidad de Familiares y Amigos de los Presos Comunes. The Peruvian Church collected 150,000 signatures to request more humane prison conditions.

32. Elías Carranza, director of the United Nations Institute for Crime Prevention and the Treatment of Offenders. Quoted on organization website, ilanud.org.

33. All these human rights organizations had specific prison projects. They were joined in their efforts by Doctors Without Borders and other groups.

34. See, for example, "¿A Alguién Le Importa?" *La Nación* (Buenos Aires) (April 27, 1997), online.

35. Amnesty International Index: AMR 19/15/99, online.

36. Nancy Cardia, *Direitos Humanos: Ausencia de cidadania e exclusão moral* (São Paulo: Comissao Justiça e Paz de São Paulo, 1995): 50.

37. *Economist* (Oct. 2, 2004), online.

38. Diane Davis, "From Democracy to Rule of Law."

39. See esp. the publications of Paulo Sergio Pinheiro, the Center's director during its formative period.

40. Bruno Paes Manso, et al., "Diadema," *Blaudel Papers* (São Paulo: Fernand Blaudel Institute), No. 36 (2005).

41. Anthony W. Pereira and Mark Unger catalogue reforms of police attempted in Argentina, Brazil, and Chile in their "Persistence of the Mano Dura" in Hite and Cesarini, eds., *Authoritarian Legacies:* 270.

42. Pereira and Unger: 284–85

43. Mark Unger, *Elusive Reform: Democracy and the Rule of Law in Latin America* (Boulder, CO: Lynne Rienner, 2002), passim.

44. Louis Anemone, a former police chief, described at length the New York methods at a security conference in Brazil in October 1999.

45. This conclusion is bolstered by the evidence presented by various authors in John Bailey and Lucía Dammert, eds., *Public Security and Police Reform in the Americas* (Pittsburgh, PA: University of Pittsburgh Press, 2006), passim. See esp.: 23 and 261.

46. Bailey and Dammert, *Public Security:* 260.

7

Torture

How do we explain such horror?
—Ricardo Lagos, President of Chile,
on presenting the Valech Report[1]

When José Aldunate acted as spokesman in 1991 for the Movement Against Torture, the Chilean group dedicated to stopping torture, he was something of a lonely figure.[2] He had been provincial superior of the Chilean Jesuits, the most prominent religious order in Chile. He had influenced the lives of many persons. However, he then headed the group with only a small number of lay members.

Chile that year had only recently returned to democratic rule after almost seventeen years of being governed by the military. Chileans felt they had to get on with their lives, except, of course, that they needed to deal with the most glaring offenses by determining who had been killed by the repressive regime. Dealing with issues of torture, such as the determination of who had been tortured or whether torture by police continued as a systematic practice, were marginal issues,[3] ones for which few had energy or, as they say among human rights activists, "fire in the belly." Aldunate had fire in the belly for the full range of human rights, not just unlawful death, but he looked like a man whose time had passed.

Beyond the comparison of torture with death and disappearance, many persons—North Americans and Chileans—think of the experience of being tortured as something one got over with the passage of time. One could look at Senator John McCain and note his humped shoulders never fully recovered from being dislocated while hanged from the rafters or whatever torture the North Vietnamese inflicted upon him. McCain obviously got on with his life. One should also note McCain never forgot. Nor did he want the United States to torture. In 2005, he was attaching amendments to bills to force the United States to abide by a no-torture policy. This chapter accounts for why torture became a major issue in Latin America although it remains a silent one in the United States. If Margaret Steinfels is correct in saying that Americans are indifferent to torture, then many Latin Americans stand in contrast to their distant neighbor to the North.[4]

The following sections take torture as a special issue in Latin American human rights, against a background of European (and some North American) concern about the inhumanity of torturing. The first section will analyze the special period beginning in the late 1960s when the state used torture against its citizens. It also deals with whether societies chose to deal with their tortured pasts. It treats at length the Valech Report from Chile that gives what is arguably the world's most complete view of a nation torturing its citizens. The second main section deals with the present-day use or suspension of torture by police and other security forces. The final section takes up mobilization by citizens against torture, a relatively new target for Latin Americans.

TORTURE DURING AUTHORITARIAN RULE

From 1964 to 1990, one after another of the Latin American countries, with few exceptions, fell under military rule and authoritarian discipline. Mexico did not have a military takeover, but Mexico had strong authoritarian rule and consequent human rights abuses through its one-party soft dictatorship until 2000.

Torture began to become a public human rights issue in Latin America in late 1969. The Brazilian military government turned hard-line late that year, becoming brutal after five years as a *dictablanda*, a soft dictatorship. The change was marked by Institutional Act 5, a presidential decree doing away with many political freedoms. Brazilian exiles argued that limiting activity in the political forum was only the tip of the iceberg. Behind the smiling faces of military leaders, in secret places, military and police were increasingly using repressive tactics. In the international sphere, Brazil's leaders boasted of the national *grandeza,* of its resources, and of Brazil's team that won the 1970 World Cup Soccer championship, endearing itself to the world with the creative, jubilant play of its team and its star, Pelé. Brazilians fleeing from this terror began showing up in Washington and New York, Santa Cruz, Bolivia, and elsewhere. They spread the word that the state was terrorizing its citizens.

Something dreadful and more or less hidden was occurring. Regional Latin American magazines that then existed and since disappeared asked: Is Torture Systematic? Was it systematic in Brazil? Probably. Was torture systematic elsewhere? When the author asked that in Cochabamba, Bolivia's third city in 1970, the response from social workers and priests working with kids who hung out in the streets was that systematic torture was creeping into policing. Little by little, torture was being applied routinely throughout Latin America.

Torture as method of control and of policing has a long history in Latin America from colonial times. Authoritarian rule was common under Iberian and Latin American governments until the 1980s, but torture as a customary measure was episodic, used especially to keep riotous situations under control, or used selectively on certain classes of persons. It was certainly not applied to all the jailed, as political prisoners, because harsh measures were thought to bring their own retribution, in time, either from victims or their families. *Venganza* (vengeance) was a common cultural trait. Jailers, using extreme measures especially in rural areas, would bring "family justice" (reparation in the shadows).

As a systematic practice, from the 1970s, two facets of torture were new. First, political prisoners were being tortured. As noted, torture was mostly reserved for common criminals, not generally persons involved in politics. Given the frequent changes of government, it did not make sense to alienate one's future partners across the congress floor or city council chambers by torturing them in their temporary imprisonment. However, imprisonment was part of the political process, moving one's opponents out of circulation by jailing or exiling them for malfeasance. Further, the political prisoners of the 1970s tended to be from social classes not used to rough handling by the servant class (police). Chile was careful to note that its Valech Commission was mandated as the National Commission on *Political* Prison and Torture.

Even countries without the military directly in the presidential palace, Colombia and Venezuela (before the drug trade was common) used torture. Torture was like a flu pandemic, afflicting the region in varying degrees. The major reason behind this was the belief that there was communist subversion being carried out and that subversion must be stopped at all costs. This Cold War frame of mind rose to the level of shared ideology, the Doctrine of National Security that affected the visions and practices of the Latin American military in varying degrees.

Whether the United States had the dominant hand in shaping this doctrine and in repressive practices remains an open question. One should not denigrate Latin Americans by believing that they could not create the National Security doctrine largely on their own at the major military command schools, notably in the Southern Cone or at Peru's CAEM (Centro de Estudios Militares). Further, military advisers in Latin America tended to be French or German.

Another aspect of torture that was new was its use in terrorizing the general populace. Few countries did this more forcibly than Uruguay. That long-standing democracy was convulsed by the new Latin American phenomenon of *urban* guerillas (Fidel Castro and Che Guevara took over Cuba through *rural* guerrilla activity). In searching for groups like the Tupamaros, Uruguayan security forces used torture on large numbers of people picked up for suspicion of subversive activity. Torture was used to gain information or was meant as a warning not to support opposition to the government. Being a small and compact country, Uruguay's use of torture was like screams in a small chamber. Through many rumors of what was happening, the cries of the tortured seemed to echo throughout the country. This new use of torture worked not only in Uruguay but also in Chile and Argentina: it created a climate of fear.

THE POLITICS OF ACCOUNTING FOR TORTURE
UNDER THE MILITARY

In 2004, twelve years after Aldunate founded the Movement Against Torture, many Chileans were fixed on their television sets as President Ricardo Lagos received the highly publicized Valech Report from a blue-ribbon commission headed by Bishop Sergio Valech. To a considerable extent, Lagos shocked the nation by revealing that some 33,000 (of a population of then eleven million) Chileans testified before the commission that they had been tortured or severely ill-treated by Chilean police or military. Lagos went on to describe the horrific manner in which torture was conducted. He also emphasized that some of those tortured were children.

After the Valech Report revelations, Chileans spent weeks psychologically processing what they had been told. Chileans torturing Chileans! This was barbarous. Chile is a democracy, and this should never have happened. The lengthy Valech Report was announced in such a way as to have maximum exposure on a Sunday night when families (Latin families prefer to watch television together) would be together and likely to carry on a discussion. Many viewers reported the strong effect the report had on them.[5]

That repression would be part of the Cold War, as interpreted by the military, was partially understandable, but Chileans did not condone the suspension of the rule of law and use of *barbarie* (barbarity). Aldunate was right: something about torture does not fit well into a democracy.

Bringing the Issue into the Public Square

How did a moribund issue became a live one? How did a marginal issue move to center stage? The context changed. Then, too, some individuals, apart from Aldunate, never gave up pressing the government for an accounting of what went on in prisons. Political environment matters greatly for social movements. Previously, the environment had included a number of factors unfavorable to pursuing the past. Loyalty to former dictator-president Augusto Pinochet was one reason. To the surprise of many North Americans, almost half the population of Chile supported the Pinochet dictatorship for its stabilizing effect and positive accomplishments. Chile made great economic advances under Pinochet. After his presidency, the general turned senator and remained a revered figure for many Chileans and for influential newspapers. More important, most Chileans lacked a historical record of what took place under the dictatorship. The media and the schools were mostly silent or silenced during the military period.[6] Thus, it was possible to believe what one wished to believe. In effect, the Chilean "pacted transition" to civilian rule acted as a stop sign to delving into the past.[7] The terms under which the presidency and the legislature during the transition were to function after the military were mostly fixed. Debate about the past was presumed to be finished, under the transition agreement.

It also looked like the Catholic Church was symbolically closing the doors to the past when in 1991, the Archbishop of Santiago closed the Vicariate of Solidarity, perhaps the main symbol of human rights advocacy in the Pinochet years.[8] Despite this assumption that many Chileans and foreigners made about the shutdown of the Vicariate, the church, in terms of individual bishops and activist religious persons, shifted to two new steps. The first was the solid establishment of the Archives and Museum of the Vicariate of Solidarity. Its records of individuals who were tortured would become important in the events that followed.

The archives are exceptionally important. They were housed on the top floor of the Santiago archdiocesan headquarters, attractively remodeled and relatively efficient in organization made possible through European church contributions. Access to the thousands of habeas corpuses written and testimonies taken by Vicariate lawyers during the dictatorship were granted to persons with ties to victims. Children were brought in groups from schools and encouraged to research what had happened to their relatives. During one visit by the author, some twelve persons, mostly young, were seen poring over yellowing folders.

In other countries with lesser honoring of the rule of law than Chile, the archives would have mysteriously burned,[9] but their existence in mid-town, on the fifth floor of a church headquarters provided a strong measure of security, in addition to the trust of a democratic people that there would be no reprisal for keeping records.

The second step made by the church was a quiet initiative to respond to the push from citizens dissatisfied with the incompleteness of the Rettig Commission. This commission had established that more than 3,000 died or disappeared under the Pinochet regime, but it did not acknowledge torture and imprisonment of many others, nor did it establish what happened to the bodies of the disappeared. It was presumed that military bureaucracies kept detailed records. So, the church offered to act as mediators at a Mesa de Diálogo. This "Dialog Round Table" was an attempt to have military and victims (of torture or of not knowing what had happened to relatives who disappeared while jailed) sit down and try to work out some understanding or reconciliation.[10]

The Chilean military, under Pinochet's continuing presidency, lasted for sixteen years, 1973–1990. The period of democratic rule was punctuated by efforts to deal with the past. By 1997, at every critical event or anniversary associated with military rule, there were demonstrations against Pinochet, or court cases were brought forward to test the legal immunity for security forces imposed in the transition. In 1997, as the twenty-fifth anniversary of the 1973 military coup approached, a flood of publications took place that included memoirs, essays, political journalism, and serious scholarship. Chile's divided historical memory was being contested. Alexander Wilde, formerly a professor at the University of Wisconsin who was observing all this while an official at the Ford Foundation in Santiago, called these "irruptions of memory," that is, "public events that break in upon Chile's national consciousness, unbidden and often suddenly, that evoke associations with the past."[11]

For the author, these events were signs of the vulnerabilities, the opportunities that give rise to social movements, or, in this case, served as occasions that breathe new life and energy into human rights movements already established. It is noteworthy that, of all the grievances about military rule, torture would serve as the theme that eventually emerged to guide society in its second major attempt to deal with the past. Torture has, in the author's view, a special incongruence with humanity, democracy, and the rule of law. In the Chilean case, torture needed to be expunged like an embedded insect from a festering wound. For the Valech Report writers, true citizenship and torture did not go together. The Bush administration and many persons in the United States have yet to embrace that belief.

In 1998, the image of Pinochet began to dissolve like a photographic image in a chemical bath. Under a European Union-backed arrest warrant, Pinochet was placed under house arrest in London, after visiting Margaret Thatcher and shopping at Harrods. For sixteen months the world and Chileans, many for the first time, read about some of the details of the cruel record of the Chilean military. Exiles from Chile, who had made known to the world in the 1970s what was occurring in Chile, dusted off their files, and these files served as the backbone of publishing the Pinochet era's record in newspapers like *The Guardian* and *El Pais* in Europe and *La Tercera* at home. Pinochet supporters were weakened by this recounting, especially by Old World authorities.

Reviving Voices

Pinochet's arrest began reviving the voices of the tortured. The *New York Times* noted, "Psychologists report that hundreds if not thousands of people . . . have begun to see therapists, to organize group therapy, to share their long-hidden horrors with spouses and children."[12] One psychologist noted that Pinochet's arrest was a great catharsis that began to break the silence.[13] The silence that was broken was not just in doctors' offices but, little by little, in the public square.

Pinochet was freed in Britain on humanitarian grounds of old-age dementia. Evidence of dementia was debatable. Chilean prosecutors pursued the possibility of a trial in Chile. Pinochet and the military institution were now vulnerable. This vulnerability drew forward those who had been tortured or in other ways affected by state repression. Day after day, victim groups and lawyers pushed the courts to strip Pinochet of his congressional immunity. While the legal proceedings dragged on, more and more of Chile's sordid history became known. A final blow to Pinochet's trustworthiness occurred when it was revealed that he and his family had amassed twenty-eight million dollars, despite a modest annual income as president or commander-in-chief. With these revelations from reporting about the Riggs Bank and other financial institutions, Pinochet faced charges of misuse of public funds, embezzlement, and tax fraud.

The myth was shattered, and the field of public opinion was open to presentation of what really happened. To have been tortured was, in 1973 through 1989, to have been presumed to be guilty of some crime. That shame could now be shed. The thrust was reversed. The tortured could be acknowledged as unjustly wronged and their reputations righted, even if injuries continued to impede physical functioning.

Chile thus entered a second major phase in dealing with its past. The first had been the 1991 Rettig Report that dealt with the deaths under government hands. As the context changed, the human rights groups that weathered the Pinochet years, pushed by Aldunate and others, sensed the vulnerability of the government and pressured for more accounting. These activists received a great boost when the United Nations named a Special Relator for Chile. The envoy, Nigel Rodley, addressed the heart of the question in his 1996 report, "The Issue of Human Rights of All Persons Who Were Submitted in Any Form to Detention or Prison, Especially to Torture or Other Inhumane Treatment."

Sensing a lack of full response to the report on the part of the government because of conservative legislators, the human rights groups took a crucial step: they organized, along with other civic groups, the Comisión Etica Contra la Tortura (Ethics Commission Against Torture).[14] This nongovernmental group included three Catholic bishops; Protestants, like Manuel Antonio Garretón; five Catholic priests; and some twenty other prominent Chileans. Much of the energy for this initiative came from persons like Paz Rojas, a psychiatrist active in the rehabilitation of torture victims.

The Comisión Etica worked diligently to craft a long document that served as the ethical and legal rationale to demand that the government act. Its *Informe* was comprehensive, including mental health questions and the torture of children. The purpose of the document was the creation of a government commission to establish a historical record of the torture that took place, assess the damage done, make reparation to those tortured, or to their families, and introduce educational materials into schools as a preventive measure against the future use of torture.

A second stream of activists organized around the Committee for the Defense of the People (CODEPU). They, too, were intent on forcing the state to face up to torture as an issue. This group on the Chilean left argued that the centrist coalition that governed Chile from Pinochet to the Socialist Lagos (1990–2000) had not dealt well with the issue of torture. CODEPU worked tirelessly, presenting Lagos with evidence of torture and pressing for criminal proceedings against security force members who tortured.[15]

Given the relatively strong position of the military in June 2001 when the Informe was presented to the government, President Lagos and congress approved a limited focus for a nonpartisan commission. Bishop Sergio Valech, the first director of the Vicariate of Solidarity, headed the group. They were instructed to establish a historical record of torture and to suggest a manner of making reparations, but identifying the agents of torture and accountability were taken off the table. (The head of the army came forward eventually with an admission of guilt for that branch of the service; other branches were mostly silent about their complicity in torture.)

José Aldunate thus achieved a major portion of what he sought. Now in his mid-80s, he could feel satisfaction for nurturing unrest until a measure of justice was done and for putting some of Chile's tortured souls to rest in peace.

What Took Place: Effective Terror in Chile

So successful was the Chilean military during its regime of state terrorism that many citizens stopped talking to one another about politics for fear of police informers. This was a great loss for many Chileans whose lives, marriages, and families were bound up in belonging to the Christian Democrat party or another of the sixteen political parties. One Chilean teacher and priest recalls the time: "We turned into a nation of whisperers. Like convicts in a prison yard, we stood, back-to-back, in the school playground, telling one another softly that somebody's father had been picked up."[16]

If Chileans believed that torture was limited to beatings with rubber hoses, the Valech Report recounted many personal histories of people subjected to near-suffocation, electric shock, and repeated beatings. Prisoners were tortured in front of other prisoners to increase the resonance of the shock.

What the Valech Report provides is a most comprehensive view of torture. It is not the world's first such view, as shall be noted later. The report also can stand as a surrogate view of what took place[17] elsewhere in Latin America. Chile was not exceptional in its cruelty.

Torture was used primarily to obtain information, and, the Valech Report said, "to inculcate profound and lasting terror in the victims and through them in anyone who had direct or indirect knowledge of the torture."[18] Ninety-four percent of the political prisoners suffered torture. Torture was calculated, tailored to fit the person. Various methods were used alternatively to increase the impact of the torture.

Among the eighteen distinct types of torture mentioned by the thousands who were tortured, repeated beatings were probably the first received and most frequently used treatment. Beatings were used routinely and indiscriminately, including on those who did not offer resistance or on those who were handcuffed or shackled. Sometimes victims were beaten repeatedly over various parts of their bodies, with guards taking turns. Not uncommonly, some fell unconscious and bleeding. Some were naked and felt totally exposed; some were hooded and felt unable to deflect blows. Damage done included impaired vision or hearing, broken teeth, malfunctioning backs, legs, or arms. Suspensions from the ceiling or wall, forced positions, electric shock to sensitive areas, faked firing squads, use of human or animal waste as food, and a catalog of other measures were used. The Chilean military apparently kept up with all the modern means to interrogate, to punish, and to terrorize.

Women made up 12 percent of the tortured. Almost all the women experienced some form of sexual violence. Three hundred sixteen experienced rape. The devastating experience of rape was sometimes magnified by the violence of the aggression and the generalized indifference of the jailers.

If torture causes lack of confidence in other human beings, sexual torture in the coarse circumstances of jails served as a special evil, with recovery a lifelong issue. The revelation that women were tortured may have caused special horror in Chileans, along with the testimony that 88 of the persons tortured were minors.

Since the scale of the repression was unknown at the time it occurred, no one knew for sure how few or how many Chileans had felt in their own flesh the sting of torture. Thirty-three thousand came forward to testify to the Valech Commission. Seven thousand claims could not be verified, and most of those are still pending. Thus, some 28,000 Chileans in a population that averaged about eleven million at the time when most torture occurred were acknowledged as having felt the lash of beatings, or worse. That amounted to about one in every 500 persons. It was certain that additional numbers, the families and friends of the victims, were deeply affected.

Chileans were chilled when they realized that torture was state policy. Moreover, torture was not an improvised phenomenon by a military thought to have taken over at the last minute because the previous president, Salvador Allende, was believed to have led the nation to the edge of economic chaos. From the first day of the coup, individual soldiers and police manhandled prisoners and then employed through the years methods of torture that could only have been planned by higher authorities. The planned quality, of course, increases fear on the part of citizens and made clear that this was state policy. Repression was pervasive in the country, being carried out at 1,132 venues that served as detention centers in the 2,400-mile-long country.

One of the small advantages of dealing with torture tardily is the greater perspective on suffering that was gained by the commission members. European and North American centers had been taking care of exiled torture victims from Latin America in relatively large numbers.[19] For some two decades these treatment centers had been publicizing the physical and psychological devastation victims had suffered. Thus, the Valech Commission members knew from these sources and from the victims themselves that torture remains in bodies that do not function well and in minds afflicted by nightmares and manifestations of traumatic stress.

Torture was viewed as causing more than psychological or physiological problems. Commission members also understood that state terror diminishes civic ideals and reduces the implicit trust among persons and the confidence that citizens of democracy should have in institutions. The sense of being a citizen, instead of merely being an inhabitant of a country, lies at the heart of democracy. Admission of guilt by the nation and a measure of reparation were expected to contribute toward mending the torn social fabric. Important, too, might be the collective resolution: never again. Easy to say, but the resolve not to use torture again is problematic.

Other Countries

The story of Brazil's dealing with its past is highlighted in *Nunca Mais* (Never Again). This was the original Portuguese title of the report of what human rights abuses the military committed during its rule. While most Brazilian readers at the time were presumed to be focused on the record of death and disappearance, the publishers of the English translation changed the title to *Torture in Brazil*. (That report was based on a million pages of military records but does not have the comprehensive view of the Valech Report.) The amount of death and disappearance of victims in Brazil was relatively small compared to other countries, so the focus of the English edition was on the main thrust of the human rights abuses of the military: the use of torture on a wide spectrum of citizens.

Torture in Brazil/Nunca Mais was a report sponsored by churches.[20] The Brazilian government never created a commission that dealt effectively with the past. Several questions remain unaddressed: recognition of the victims and perpetrators and reparation for the past and continued use or suspension of torture by security forces in a democratic setting.

For some in Brazil, such as Frei Betto and Frei Tito, torture remains like a rotted corpse still hanging on a tree. Betto is a well-published Brazilian writer whose *Batismo de Sangue* (Baptism by Blood) is in its thirteenth edition. In the work Betto, who is a Dominican brother[21] and suffered torture while a university student in the 1970s, keeps revising his history of abuses as more facts are made known. Brazil's governments years after the events have yet to offer recognition of what took place. If that occurs, the process may grant rest to Frei Tito, a Dominican brother-student, who committed suicide after torture in Brazil and exile in France, unable to shake the voices that tormenters put in his head.

Marcos Arruda, an economist with dozens of published books, suffered imprisonment and torture for some months in Brazil. When he asked Brazil's former president why the government did not deal with its history of torture and death, Fernando Henrique Cardoso said that no congressman had initiated such legislation.[22] In other words, not enough pressure from below and no opportune occasion existed by which the government would have to act.

Uruguay, the country with perhaps the highest per capita numbers of imprisoned and tortured political prisoners, refused at least until 2002 to begin to establish either a record of torture or other injustices under military rule or to determine the guilt of any parties. In human rights circles, Uruguay became known as an "Island of Impunity." Finally in October 2002, the Peace Commission created by President Jorge Battlle recognized for the first time that the state had killed 26 persons under torture. The commission also found that 40 citizens were kidnapped and killed in Uruguay and another 170 Uruguayans kidnapped and killed in Argentina.

Does government and widespread public recognition of torture as evil, as in the case of Chile, have an effect in eliminating torture in the time of democratic rule, in the everyday practice of police and prison officials? Did *nunca mas/mais* really mean never again in Brazil?

PRESENT-DAY USE OF TORTURE BY POLICE AND PRISONS

Torture appears to be diminishing in Chile, except in prisons where occasional torture seems to be related to overcrowding. However, prisons in other countries form a major arena for the present-day practice of torture. (Since the majority of prisoners are now mostly common criminals or drug mules, one might expect that mobilization against torturing them would be nearly impossible.)

Nunca mais proved not to be true in Brazil. While, in general, the government respected the rights of its citizens, police and prison officials committed serious abuses. "Torture by police and prison guards remained a serious and widespread problem," the US State department reports.[23] More than 2,500 allegations of torture were made in a fifteen-month period ending in January 2004, and this was probably an under-reporting. Brazilians could believe that progress was made in urban areas since torture took place mostly in rural areas. The victims were typically young, poor, Afro-Brazilian men from less-developed areas. However, irrespective of place, torture continues in the FEBEM juvenile detention centers.

In Latin America's other large country, Mexico, torture is still regarded as a major problem. This is an aspect of policing and imprisonment, already described. In other countries, the use of torture by police varies from occasional to regularly occurring. Torture in prisons is a major problem. Prisons are the venues for the worst human rights violations in the region. Further description of individual countries and the extent of torture violations are treated in sections below dealing with country efforts to mobilize against torture.

More than merely calling attention to traditional use of torture and the continuation of authoritarian policing and prison control, Brazilian, Mexican, and other Latin American human rights advocates are mobilizing to do something about torture in their countries.

MOBILIZING AGAINST TORTURE

Transnational Movement

Citizens of the United States may be surprised at how strongly Europeans, with the exception of Great Britain, feel about torture. The agreement in the European Community is expressed in the European Union's regime, the Convention Against Torture and Other Cruel, Inhuman or Degrading Torture or Punishment. More important for our purposes, the transnational mobilization, especially from Europe, against the practice of torture has advanced to a high level. Some 266 human rights organizations, most of them regional or local, form a basis for fighting against torture in a network organized by the World Organization Against Torture. This organization works to provide rapid response to urgent situations and to act as a prime source of information to the United Nations and to the Inter-American Commission on Human Rights. The World Organization started with 48 organizations in 1986, and its impressive growth indicates increasing interest in many parts of the world, generally speaking without US leadership, or, worse, disdain on the part of the United States. Among human rights sections of the

United Nations an influential agency for Latin America has been the Committee Against Torture (CAT), as will be noted in individual country efforts to deal with torture.

An international think tank, the Association for the Prevention of Torture (APT), was founded by Swiss philanthropist Jean-Jacques Gautier to back up the transnational movement against torture. APT has sent missions to several Latin American countries, including Brazil and Mexico, often working in tandem with the Inter-American Institute for Human Rights and local human rights groups. Uruguay made special use of APT in recent reform efforts, as will be noted.

Networks of Transnational Centers for the Victims of Torture. That torture has become a mainline issue in human rights is due to a considerable degree to two to three decades of awareness of the practice of torture. This consciousness raising was enhanced through centers for the treatment of victims of torture in Europe and the United States. For some time, these centers had to exist offshore, since countries that tortured did not want to acknowledge the damage done.

The Center for Victims of Torture (CVT) in Minneapolis was the first to be founded in the United States and third in the world. Personnel at CVT provided rehabilitation for victims, but they also conducted research on torture, its effects, and treatment. Unlike traditional health facilities, it moved into advocacy for policy initiatives to benefit survivors and to end the practice of torture.

As Turkey sought full admission in the EU and faced objections to its entry in part because of the somewhat unfettered use of torture, CVT coordinated a symposium in Turkey on a key theme for CVT, new tactics in human rights. This was but one of many of its action initiatives.

Further, CVT makes up only one link in the International Rehabilitation Council for Torture Victims (IRCT), a network of some 200 centers. By 2005, these centers for the rehabilitation of torture victims had spread from the North Atlantic countries to most of the world. In these centers health professionals had treated almost 35,000 affected persons. In centuries past, victims would have had to fend for themselves. Now medicine and communication have come together to extend the kindness of strangers. Many of the centers are also trying to hold up a mirror to national and international societies in which they can view the effects of torture. As much as possible, this effort is aimed at reducing torture as an isolating experience.

As the grip of military governments weakened in the late 1980s, Latin Americans felt emboldened to organize rehab centers on their own soil. (Remember that countries not only torture, they sometimes threaten the victims of torture, so they will neither call attention to themselves nor publish their histories.)[24] The centers have created a regional network, Red Latinoamericana y del Caribe de Instituciones contra la Tortura y Otras Violaciones de los Derechos Humanos. This regional network forms another link in the chain of the IRCT transnational network against torture.

Religion and Torture. This relationship is coming to the foreground. Its history is better understood by Europeans than North Americans. In a word, torture was part of

Western European civilization and has been repudiated in contemporary times. This is reflected in the "new" Catholic Catechism, as contrasted to the thin version older Catholics memorized. Catholics now read that torture was part of the tradition of the Roman Empire, that legitimate governments were seen as using torture to maintain order and to punish criminals, and that view has changed: "In recent times it has become evident that these cruel practices were neither necessary for public order, nor in conformity with the legitimate rights of the human person. On the contrary, these practices led to ones even more degrading. It is necessary to work for their abolition. We must pray for the victims and their tormentors."[25]

The first Mexican group specifically focused on the abolition of torture is a branch of the Association of Christians Against Torture (ACAT). This group, with British roots similar to Amnesty International, owed its impetus to Peter Berenson, the founder of Amnesty International. Mexicans opened a small center of ACAT in Mexico City and opened a reception center for the victims of torture and their families in the state of Guerrero where guerrilla activity and torture as a government response have been frequent occurrences. Christians, especially European ones, have joined "secular" human rights movements, without feeling the need to have a specifically Christian group, and have argued that groups like ACAT fragment the movement.

Arts and Torture. Latin American and foreign novelists, playwrights, and visual artists have helped to make torture a special issue in ways that were not common before military rule. Perhaps the best known scene for North American audiences is Sigourney Weaver, a victim of torture and abuse, turning the tables on Ben Kingsley, the doctor present at her torture. The film *Death and the Maiden* about torture in Chile had much more success as a 1991 play in London and, perhaps, New York.[26] The problem with fiction is that it tends to create a distancing of the issue for audiences, as the *The New Times has noted.*

Several countries have vibrant local theater, but mounting plays about repression only slowly occurred within the countries. Rodrigo Pérez was one of the first Chilean playwrights to present torture as a central theme in January 2003.[27] In Guatemala, traveling theater groups with native, untrained actors have fanned through the country in an effort to aid communities to break the silence about what happened. In another effort for Guatemala, the Danish journalist Lotte Holmen and collaborators created a website, Para Nunca Olvidar, where one can hear interviews that Holmen conducted through the years with victims.[28] The site also presents drawings of the Danish artist Bjørn Bie, who lived in Guatemala seventeen years and portrayed scenes of what happened in remote communities.

Contemporary Efforts against Torture

Most Latin American countries where torture was common now have an organization dedicated to victims of torture. Varying in influence from country to country, these institutions form a backbone for the current efforts to acknowledge torture as a human rights issue.

Chile. If one had to choose among these sixteen centers for the most courageous or most effective, CINTRAS (Centro de Salud Mental y Derechos Humanos) in Chile would be high on the list. CINTRAS and persons associated with it furnished a major impetus for the various steps leading to the Valech Commission and also for pushing for even more accountability for torture than Chile or the Valech Commission has provided. Other Chilean organizations working against torture have already been noted.

Mexico. Pressure was put on Mexico by the United States and Canada in the run-up period to the formulation and signing of the North American Free Trade Agreement (NAFTA) that took effect January 1, 1994. Progress in the twenty-first century was stalled in Mexico's human rights endeavors, especially in regard to policing, prisons, and specifically torture. Mexico's main coalition of human rights organizations lined up on torture and moved it from the margins to closer to center stage.

The United Nations Committee Against Torture (CAT) noted in its 1997 report that "torture continues to be systematically practiced in Mexico."[29] CAT's report in 2003 was the same and added that no conviction about the use of torture has been made. In 2005, when President Vicente Fox stated that in the last two years there had been only one complaint about torture and that complaint had been resolved, the human rights movement Todos los Derechos para Todos called Fox a "liar," unusually strong language in public. The movement stated, "Torture continues as a systematic practice in Mexico."[30]

However, long-term observers could note that progress in confronting torture in Mexico has been made in several regards. Advances have been made in the widening of political space and the lessening of authoritarian reprisal whereby Todos los Derechos para Todos was free to speak up, including the embarrassment of the president over his faulty human rights record.[31] In the years when Mexico was in the grip of authoritarian governments, standing up to the president was virtually unknown. Then, too, the fifty-five groups that make up Todos los Derechos have clearly made torture a priority among the many human rights issues they might have chosen to emphasize. Also, voices of international torture-monitoring agencies, such as the United Nations, are being heard by the Mexican government in ways that were not common twenty years ago.

Brazil. The Movement for Human Rights (MNDH) brought about a creative innovation, Torture SOS, a hotline administered by MNDH for reporting allegations of torture. Another group, the Christian Association for the Abolition of Torture became involved in attempts to end torture in São Paulo state prisons. The latter association is loosely related to the Mexican group just mentioned. In Brazil, probing into torture often leads into investigating extrajudicial killing and then into fears for the safety of investigators, for example, Isabel Peres, the coordinator of the Brazilian branch of ACT.

Brazilians have a more fully developed response to torture than many countries, at least in a symbolic sense (a sphere in which Brazilians excel). The Movimento Tortura

Nunca Mais (MTNM) split with the Commission on the Dead and the Politically Disappeared in 1986 to address the broader issues of torture. MTNM at the time founded major regional branches in Rio, São Paulo, Brasília, Porto Alegre, and Pernambuco.

Uruguay. To a great extent the issue of dealing with the national memory of torture has melded into the issue of torture as a contemporary legal issue and as a problem occurring in prisons. It is noteworthy that when Uruguay's new Socialist government made prison reform a top priority, the group that the government invited to advise them was the Association for the Prevention of Torture, not a generic human rights group. The association's recommendations included criminalization of torture in the criminal code, in addition to a prison ombudsman. The national press, important for support of reforms, gave the visit wide publicity.

One of the principal activists in both efforts was the Jesuit priest, Luis Pérez Aguirre (known by most as Perico), who had been tortured while imprisoned for reasons never made clear. To the author, Pérez Aguirre appeared in a 2000 interview to be what one imagined to be a suffering soul, but one who had turned his considerable energies into human rights education. He was killed in 2001 while riding a bike, run over by a bus.

Perico would be pleased that the branch organization he founded, Service for Peace and Justice (SERPAJ),[32] was part of the NGOs that matched up with UN Commission against Torture in late 2005 in an effort to implement the Protocol Against Torture that Uruguay signed in 1985 but never implemented until 2005. SERPAJ was joined by other long-suffering groups, the Institute for Legal and Social Studies and, of course, the ever-active Mothers and Relatives of the Uruguayan Detained-Disappeared.

The UN commission's presence serves as a reminder that the Uruguayan government must, under the protocol, create watchdog organizations to guard against torture in prisons and to join in a worldwide effort to abolish torture.

Venezuela. The oldest democracy in Latin America was buffeted by spillover from the war on drugs in the Andes, especially in rough frontier near Lara. Venezuelan security forces fought drug gangs with extrajudicial killings and torture. Torture has been a problem in Venezuela for a long time in the treatment of prison inmates. Indeed, prisons seemed the single worst human rights blight in the country.

While there is no full movement against torture in Venezuela, two groups have taken the small, arduous steps that help control torture in the country. They document cases of torture through their professional staff of lawyers and legal assistants. They make the cases part of the public record. PROVEA established itself as the best known Venezuelan NGO dealing in human rights protection and education. PROVEA makes contact with transnational bodies, such as the United Nations' various human rights offices, more effective in many ways, especially when the government is reluctant to live up to its international regime agreements. It also serves as a liaison with government agencies and documents cases of torture and ill treatment that make government denial less likely. Red de Apoyo also has a moderately strong voice, one that reflects its grassroots origins. The network derived from small Christian communities and neighborhood groups that grew out of frustration from a flooding disaster and governmental inaction. Red de Apoyo provides rehabilitation for some torture victims and documentation of the abuse they suffered.

Colombia. Probably Columbia is the Latin American country with the most cases of torture by security forces, especially those involved in fighting a drug "war" enlarged through very large amounts of aid from the United States in a flawed initiative called Plan Colombia. Very little national activity has been mobilized against torture, although mental health workers in 1992 formed AVRE, a group to assist victims affected by the violence of civil war in the country. These efforts, while inadequate, keep the issue of torture alive within the influential Universidad Nacional de Colombia.

Argentina. The country broke a legal logjam when the legislature annulled laws giving immunity to the armed forces. Some 100 security force persons have been charged with crimes, including torture. Argentina had yet to present a comprehensive view of what occurred to those imprisoned and tortured. Again, no triggering opportunity for social movement creation was seized. Still, tortured Argentines have been restless and their experience is kept alive by diffuse efforts, as noted below.

One group dealing with torture is the Argentine Team for Psychosocial Work and Investigation (EATIP), founded in 1990. Since Argentina has the highest ratio of psychoanalysts and psychotherapists per person in the world,[33] it is not surprising that these health professionals would be involved in indirectly keeping alive what might be described as a collective memory of torture. EATIP is headed by four psychiatrists. The group grew from the same team that offered psychological assistance to the Mothers of the Plaza de Mayo and is based in the "peoples' university" run by the Mothers.

When Patricia Isasa returned from exile in England and felt the need to determine the places where she was tortured and the persons who imprisoned and tortured her as an adolescent, she was met at every corner by stonewalling and denial. Indeed, her quest threatened lower- and middle-level persons still in power. Presumably her membership in CGT, a main workers union, gave her some protection. As an architect with her own studio, she had the creativity to develop her own documentary, "El Cerco." If she could not be heard at home, she carried the message about torture outside Argentina. In 1995, Isasa went through the United States on a national speaking tour. It did not take much imagination to jump from scenes of Police Station 1 in Santa Fe, Argentina, where Isasa was tortured, to Abu Ghraib.

CONCLUSION

In sum, Latin American human rights groups have made torture a special issue, worthy of national attention. The practice of torture has been part of Latin America's history (as it has been part of western civilization), but the use of torture or other inhumane treatment intensified during military and authoritarian rule during the 1970s and 1980s. Chileans have led the way through a national effort to account for the use of torture during sixteen years of military rule. Their Valech Commission may be the only such effort worldwide to focus on torture. Torture continues as an occasional practice by some police forces and may be diminishing. However, torture or other inhumane conduct continues to be practiced in prisons, at least on an occasional basis.

Torture has become a major human rights issue in Latin America. To counter the practice of torture, human rights groups have bonded together in a growing transnational movement. Both centers for victims and religion have added new dimensions to the movement. Human rights advocates have made a number of national efforts to reduce torture and inhumane punishment. These efforts bring Latin America closer to an antitorture ethos becoming prevalent in Europe and farther away from the United States where torture is a silent issue.[34]

NOTES

1. "Chile torture victims win payout," *BBC News* (Nov. 29, 2004), online.

2. The group was called Movimiento Contra la Tortura Sebastián Acevedo, named after a lesser-known person, a construction worker in Concepción, who died in 1983 as a suicide protesting military repression of his children. The choice of an ordinary person may have lessened interest in the movement but kept alive the view of ordinary persons protesting the cruelties of the Pinochet regime.

3. See, for example, Nigel S. Rodley, "Torture and Conditions of Detention," in Juan E. Mendez, et al., eds, *The (Un)Rule of Law and the Underprivileged in Latin America* (Notre Dame, IN: University of Notre Dame Press, 1999): 28 and accompanying endnote 6.

4. *The Economist* attributes a change in American attitudes toward torture to having suffered "the world's most horrific attack" on September 11, 2001 in "Special Report on Torture" (Jan. 11, 2003): 18. Andrew Romano traces the evolution of the change in "How Terror Led America toward Torture," *Newsweek* (Nov. 21, 2005), online.

5. The impact of the Valech Report has not, to the author's satisfaction, been measured.

6. The Pinochet government took over universities and at least some high schools, placing military officers in charge.

7. For rules of the game after authoritarian regimes, see Hite and Cesarini, *Authoritarian Legacies:* 8ff.

8. For a preliminary history see: *Moral Opposition to Authoritarian Rule in Chile, 1973–90,* by Pamela Lowden (Oxford, England: St. Anthony Press, 1996).

9. See questions of files in Ginger Thompson, "Mildewed Police Files May Hold Clues to Atrocities in Guatemala," *The New York Times* (Nov. 21, 2005): 1.

10. The attempt at mediation by the Catholic Church was something new in Chile and was employed elsewhere, notably Argentina.

11. Alexander Wilde, "Irruptions of Memory: Expressive Politics in Chile's Transition to Democracy," *Journal of Latin American Studies* 31, 2 (May 1999): 473–500.

12. Clifford Kraus, "Shadows of Torment: Pinochet Reviving Voices of the Tormented," *The New York Times* (Jan. 3, 2000), web archives.

13. Ibid.

14. Two groups that were central to organizing the Comisión Etica were CODEPU (see below) and CINTRAS, the latter a group that had worked on the rehabilitation of victims of torture.

15. Committee for the Defense of the People's *Preinforme*, Dec. 10, 2002; *Segundo Informe*, Dec. 10, 2003; *Tercer Informe*, Dec. 10, 2004.

16. Interview with Erwin Fonseca, June 14, 1994. Santiago, Chile.

17. Ranking genocides and tortured countries is reprehensible in the author's view, although some universities have indulged themselves in the practice.

18. Valech: 255.

19. Information available at www.irct.org.

20. The process of compiling the report and its publication was supported largely by the mainline Protestant World Council of Churches and the Catholic Archdiocese of São Paulo.

21. Betto is a nom de plume; his given name is Carlos Alberto Libânio Christo.

22. Public discussion, Watson Center, Brown University, October 19, 2005.

23. US Department of State, Annual Report of Human Rights, online.

24. Turkey was reported in 2005 to be threatening victims of torture.

25. No. 2298 *Catechism of the Catholic Church*.

26. The New York production was marred by a controversy over casting of non-Latinos.

27. "Rodrigo Pérez Retrata la Tortura," *La Tercera* (Jan. 17, 2003), online.

28. See para-nunca-olvidar.org.

29. Committee Against Torture, A/52/44, paragraphs: 153–70.

30. Todos los Derechos para Todos, *Boletín* 09/2005 (March 31, 2005): 2.

31. See the critique of the Fox administration in the exposition of the Centro de Derechos Humanos Miguel Augustín Pro, "La Situación de los Derechos Humanos en México," online, no date given.

32. SERPAJ was founded in Argentina by the Nobel prizewinner Adolfo Pérez Esquivel.

33. "Psychiatrists See Income Plummet," *Psychiatric News* 37, 10 (May 17, 2002): 15.

34. A noteworthy exception in the United States is the San Francisco-based Center for Justice and Accountability that has been working with victims of torture through rehabilitation and through bringing perpetrators to trial.

8

Corruption

Corruption takes food from the mouth of the poor.

—Honduran saying

The trouble (with a reformer) is that he can't see no difference between honest and dishonest graft.

—George Washington Plunkett of Tammany Hall[1]

Corruption has become a priority among human rights violations in Latin America. This evil would not have been listed twenty years ago. Death and disappearance were the focus of human rights groups then. This is not a isolated fight from the grassroots, and Latin American governments acknowledge this as a key issue. Further, the United Nations, the Organization of American States, the World Bank, and the Latin American Catholic Church have thrown their weight behind the struggle. Why this shift occurred and how the issue pertains to human rights is addressed in this chapter.

Corruption has affected Latin America for centuries. Now, along with some other regions of the world, Latin American human rights groups have made corruption a special target. In a word, corruption has increased in scale due to new opportunities and so, too, have efforts to combat corruption. The Catholic Church, especially in the person of Cardinal Oscar Rodríguez Maradiaga, has thrown its weight into this struggle since the mid-1990s.

The following sections take up, first, why corruption is now an issue and how corruption has been part of Latin American history and culture; second, what is being done and by which organizations; and lastly, Latin American efforts within a transnational framework.

FIRST STOP SIGNS

Perhaps the first sign that it would not be corruption as usual occurred in Brazil in the early 1990s. After more than twenty years of military rule, one of Brazil's first elected presidents, the telegenic Fernando Collor de Mello, became the first president in the history of Latin America to be impeached. The reason was corruption. Public opinion became a major reason that a typically fractious and timid Brazilian congress was forced into acting.[2]

If Collor remained a singular case it would have been possible to say that Brazil was an aberration in the region, but the Collor case was quickly followed by Venezuelans throwing out their president, Carlos Andrés Pérez,[3] and Guatemalans forcing president Jorge Antonio Serrano Elías out of the presidential palace. Corruption or not following constitutional order was no longer tolerable. Human rights groups were in the forefront of demanding their removal.

Seeing this new intolerance, Carlos Menem, the once-popular president of Argentina, dropped out of the two-person presidential run-off election in 2003, while leading in the first round of voting, apparently afraid of facing evidence of wrongdoing in secret arms deals with Ecuador. The Andean countries, Peru, Ecuador, and Bolivia in the 1990s forced presidents out of office—no news there, except that the threats of judicial procedures against the presidents had the strength of robust democratic convictions about abuse of power from the grassroots instead of historically embedded indifference or fatalism. Mexico saw its once-strong president, Carlos Salinas de Gotari, who guided the country into the North American Free Trade Agreement, fall into disgrace when it became clear in 1995 that he and his family enriched themselves through corruption. While Salinas went off to Ireland in disgrace, Arnoldo Alemán, the former president of Nicaragua, was not as fortunate and was sentenced to twenty years in prison for fraud and embezzlement. Also in prison was Ladimiro Montesinos, the chief architect of corruption under former Peruvian president Alberto Fujimori, sentenced to fifteen years for extortion. Finally, whatever aura former Chilean president Augusto Pinochet had fell like dust from a statue of a hero, once it was revealed that he and his family enriched themselves with some twenty-eight million dollars.[4] The list of disgraced ex-presidents continues to grow, reaching even Costa Rica.

Those instances show the changing public perception of corruption in Lain America. Several facets of Latin America facing up to corruption are new. Most of the countries are recent democracies, forged out of reaction to military or authoritarian dictatorship. In the process of democratization, major debates on the shape of future governance took place. Perhaps for the first time, many persons began to believe that a way forward with lessened corruption was possible. In part, this belief was based on seeing what their own actions could accomplish. In the 1980s and 1990s, they created better neighborhoods, forced the government to be more responsive to their needs, and advocated and advanced basic human rights. In a word, Latin America had become in many places a movement society or at least had the makings of a civil society it did not possess, say, in 1970. Evidence shows that there are some one million civil society organizations in Latin America.[5] Many of them are devoted to improving good governance and thereby the lives of ordinary people at the grassroots.

The classic example of the awakening took place in Mexico after the 1985 Mexico City earthquake. When the government faltered in its response to massive and serious problems, people began organizing at the grassroots to dig through the ruins and to rebuild. Many Mexicans underwent something like a conversion from the fatalism of depending on the government to fix things to reliance on their own efforts. The symbol of this change was Super Barrio, the paunchy middle-aged man dressed as a Mexican Superman, who went from barrio to barrio preaching neighborhood organizing.

People at the grassroots now have a twenty- to thirty-year history of activism that includes some impressive accomplishments. After a year of interviewing Brazilian activists, Jeffrey Rubin said he was "repeatedly struck by the sense of achievement of the people.... They have seen their work consistently advance, despite harsh repression and setbacks." Further, he was impressed by "the vital character of their debates." In Chile, Argentina, Bolivia, and Peru, the author of this volume observed similar vital debates and would only add that he was struck by the number of late-teen and twenty-year-olds assuming full membership in the civil society-activist groups. The age-replacement factor for leadership is also positive in Brazil's largest sociopolitical movement—that of the Landless—treated in a separate chapter herein.

The second factor, a negative one, is the new opportunities and a growing magnitude of the enrichment possible in the process of globalization. One aspect of this process was extensive privatization. As countries adjusted to free-market capitalism, they privatized state enterprises, such as phone companies and airlines. In some countries, former state enterprises fell like goodies into the hands of a favored few insiders, without competition or transparency. Not only did a globalized economy in general bring large opportunities for illicit enrichment, national institutional sources of corruption increased in post-authoritarian situations.[6] Transnational sources of investment money and "favors" add new and often secret sources of enrichment. The size of development projects mean billions of dollars available.

Privatization was an especially vexing opportunity for enrichment. Latin American economies, for the most part, were statist. The state sold off public enterprises such as television networks, phone companies, and public utilities through a corruptible process of privatization. At what price and to whom was not always transparent. When countries divested themselves of telephone companies, airlines, television stations, and other enterprises, it was likened in Mexico to a birthday party game, la piñata, with a papier-mâché figure. The figure, whose belly was laden with candy, was broken by a blow of a stick, and the goodies fell at the feet of the invited few who scooped up the favors. So, too, were Mexican fortunes made by the favored in-crowd. Sometimes foreigners were the favored beneficiaries, as when Venezuela cut loose CANTV, Viasa airline, and several large hotels at undervalued prices in the 1980s.

Even one of the cleanest countries was affected by new global investments.[7] Costa Ricans felt they stood head and shoulders above other Central Americans in terms of honesty in government. Transparency International ratings backed them up.[8] Presidents serve one term in Costa Rica, and it used to be said that when they exited the presidency, they returned to whatever economic status they possessed before the presidency. That seems to be true of the senior José "Pepe" Figueres, the father of contemporary Costa Rica, and of Oscar Arias, the Nobel architect of peace in the region. However, Costa Ricans were stunned when, within months, not one but rather three former presidents, including the son of Pepe Figueres, were accused of taking money illicitly. For the most part, the sums involved were not large by international standards, and at least one case was borderline, that of acting as a consultant to a government-awarded contract. Globalization had brought Costa Ricans opportunities for enrichment that did not exist before. Public trust had been broken. To his credit, Costa Rican President Abel Pacheco de la Espriella acted decisively, even when it was not easy to do so. (He acted against "his own class," it was said.)

A third new element in the contemporary situation of corruption is changes made in the United States and Europe. The September 11, 2001, and other terrorist attacks brought oversight changes that made it more difficult to hide assets. As a rule of thumb, money is laundered better in Northern countries than the Southern ones.[9] Hence, money flowed through the Florida banks south of the Miami River and through District of Columbia institutions, including the Riggs Bank.

In the United States, through the Patriot Act, government officials exercised oversight of the American assets of foreigners, including those suspected of corruption in their own countries. These investigations brought to light funds associated with presidents of Nicaragua, Ecuador, and Guatemala. The Patriot Act also granted American officials another weapon: the ability to deny visas to the United States. Officials thereupon called attention to tainted former presidents of Colombia and Panama through denial of visas.

Lastly, empirical research conducted in Latin America since the late 1990s shows there are practical ways that do reduce corruption. Public awareness campaigns that enlist the general public in the fight against corruption, along with other measures, are effective tools.[10] Combating corruption is more than a naive wish or hopeless quixotic enterprise.

Historical View

What is now viewed as corruption—here defined as the abuse of public office or trust for private gain—was often seen by Mediterranean cultures, Spanish, Portuguese, and French, as entitlements. Even contemporary French government officials expected to have access to prime apartments in Paris for family or mistresses. Every month into the late 1990s, a bank truck pulled up to the offices of French government officials with bags of thousands of francs to be used as discretionary and nonaccountable funds by cabinet ministers. As the Crown often could not provide salaries in earlier days, their officials were kept alive and well-dressed by dipping into funds. Likewise, contemporary

Brazilian and other high-level officials expected to have a "black box" in their desks with discretionary funds.

Corruption is not a formless evil on the science-fiction channel. At the level of the ordinary citizen, corruption takes shape at the request, often implicit but well-understood, for payment of a fee to officials for services rendered or penalties avoided. Police, school staff, and governmental bureaucrats receiving poverty-level wages hoped to be aided toward a reasonable level of income by what has colorful names, such as *mordida* (the bite), or *muñeca* (money placed under the wristwatch or bracelet). How this scourge is, or is not, being contained will be addressed below.

Two symbols emerged out of recent history that point to the changes toward intolerance of corruption by public officials. The clinking of cutlery against glass became common in the eastside restaurants of Caracas, a signal that patrons use to indicate the unwelcome presence of high-ranking civil servants, military officers, and representatives of the government or public institutions they suspect of sharing in government corruption. The tinkling noise may start at one table or another, but soon enough other guests join in. The purpose of the ensuing racket, which everyone in the restaurant is aware of, is to make the objectionable officials feel despised. This kind of action recurs on the streets via the banging of pots and pans in what has become a sign of rejection in Latin American society. The banging of pots and pans became a central feature of protests in Chile in the 1980s and again in Argentina after the turn of the last century.

Views of Corruption by Disciplines

Analyzing corruption has become a lively academic enterprise. The discourse about corruption has taken place at an unusual speed, driven by scholars on both sides of the Atlantic communicating in journals and papers widely available in print and on the web and through the World Bank website. Not all academics took a dim view of corruption. Perhaps to the surprise of the unlettered, several serious scholars, including Samuel Huntington, pointed out the positive aspects of bribes and other aspects of corruption.[11] It was affirmed that bribes were like stimulants making sluggish bureaucracies act when they would not have acted, even in a good cause. Other reasons have been alleged, as well.

In general, though, economists argue that corruption reduces investment incentives, increases transaction costs, and results in reduced economic growth. In one of the most extensive efforts to estimate bribery costs for one aspect of corruption, government services, grassroots pollsters interviewed heads of households. The investigators estimated that corruption in the use of public services cost Bolivians, most of them very poor, the equivalent of US $115 million a year.[12] The survey included a full range of forty-two public services. Each household was estimated as having paid US $50 a year in bribes, a sum equal to 90 percent of a monthly salary. No wonder then that economists at the World Bank have identified corruption as the single greatest obstacle to economic and social development.

Political scientists more recently have argued that corruption erodes the legitimacy of governments, the major pillar of democracy. Mitchell Seligson, through extensive research in nine countries, showed that corruption does erode the legitimacy of governance, a precious characteristic in the new democracies of Latin America.[13] Legitimacy is needed for governmental system stability. Human rights activists have argued that corruption in government basically steals from the poor the resources that should be going into providing for their health, education, and other services.

The same argument has been made forcibly by the Catholic Church, especially by Cardinal Oscar Rodríguez of Honduras. The Latin American Bishops Conference (CELAM) began in the late 1990s to lay a foundation that would became a major thrust of the church. In its "Declaración ética contra la corruption," the church in 1997 analyzed the situation of public and private corruption.[14] National bishops' conferences followed this lead. The Central American bishops were soon described by *La Prensa* (Honduras) as making anticorruption efforts "the new battle horse of the Catholic Church."[15] The Ecuadoran bishops in 1998 made a strong appeal from scripture and the social teaching of the church.[16] The Argentine bishops took a sharp stand in 2001, calling corruption the evil that undermines the country.[17] The Mexican bishops in 2004 proposed a five-point plan to combat corruption in the country.[18] While these efforts may be regarded by secular observers as puff pieces, others see their efforts as useful in creating a national discussion about corruption as will be seen.

The perspective of economists and older political scientists, for the most part, tends to focus on the institutional level; the perspective of human rights activists, the Church and more recently, political scientists emphasizes the individual and the resources that are supposed to be dispensed to them by institutions without coercion.[19]

The Victims of Corruption

The latter perspective has been explored by Mitchell Seligson: the individual as victim of corruption. A political scientist working originally at the University of Pittsburgh and then at Vanderbilt, Seligson created LAPOP to report on opinion polls he conducted. This empirical research opened a perspective beyond the endless essays about Latin American corruption. Through tireless public opinion polling especially in Mexico, Central America, and Colombia, Seligson and collaborators conducted research into who has been directly affected by corrupt transactions. In 2004, they focused in nine countries on corruption-victimization in the workplace and in four government services: health, courts, schools, and local government. This valuable research yielded information about the frequency with which bribes occurred and about the venues in which they occurred.[20]

In some ways the view that they provide is both better and worse than one might have expected. Some countries, such as war-torn Colombia, have a good deal fewer victims of corruption than other countries, and the overall averages for the nine countries are a good deal better than many developing countries. However, to find that the school system is the venue of the most bribery was shocking to Seligson and likely would be to most observers. One hates to dwell on the implications of children being socialized in a system where corruption is endemic. (In the worst case, Ecuador, almost one in four parents reported school bribes.) Municipal bribery was almost as high as school bribery and court bribery, followed by lower rates of bribery in the workplace and health service. The percentages ranged from 10.6 percent of Latin Americans who were victims of school bribery to 7.5 percent who reported being asked for health service bribes.

The differences among countries were significant. Among the nine countries studied, Mexicans and Ecuadorians were subjected to more corruption than citizens of the other countries studied. Regarding all kinds of bribes, one-fifth of the Mexican population experienced some form of bribery; Ecuadorians experienced almost the same level. In other countries, only 3 to 10 percent said they were similarly approached. The majority of Latin Americans in the study did not report being asked for bribes.

Seligson shows the evil of corruption. In contrast to the right that citizens have for the expectation of fair and equal distribution of goods from the state, instead of free and uncoerced delivery of service from public servants, citizens receive unjust treatment and coercion. Corruption thus strikes at the heart of the rule of law and due process as foundations of democracy. Further, corruption induces a fear that is a kind of low-level terrorism or at least coercion that reduces the kind of trust needed to oil the workings of good governance. A case could be made that police and bureaucrats are also victims in the sense that they do not receive income from wages sufficient for their support and that of their families. Bribes, slightly similar to tips to waiters, are seen as part of their wages, perhaps rewarding the zealous more than the lazy officers. Beyond the interpersonal aspects, governmental corruption also reduces the supply of resources for all and hurts the weak and vulnerable most. The billions of pesos that have been funneled into private hands is indeed grand theft from the people.

THE FERTILE GROUND

Framing corruption in terms of human rights has been a change for many Latin Americans from the time when they accepted corruption as an inevitable part of the cultural landscape. Human rights discourse offers newly-found resistance to violations of various political and economic rights that are beyond the so-called first-generation rights. Human rights activists, community leaders, and active participants in civil society—many, not all—have engaged in an examination of the cultural roots of corruption.

Among other institutions, churches have furnished compelling reasons to regard the culture of corruption as an unacceptable part of Latin American society. The Catholic

Church attempted to present its point of view within a national dialogue about good governance in several countries as well as for the whole region. Anticorruption efforts will probably not take hold until a dialogue among citizens about corruption takes place in the public square and some consensus is reached about corruption as an evil. This is in contrast to efforts emanating from the World Bank—despite all its useful reports on corruption since the early 1990s—that are fundamentally focused on treating symptoms. Informants in various countries told the author that the church's position in the national dialogue and its voice in national society was a positive influence toward controlling corruption. In one of the few grassroots surveys, Bolivians rate the church rather highly (4.5 on a scale of 7) in anticorruption efforts.[21]

National dialogues about corruption are taking place. Anticorruption public opinion continues as a steady force of resistance in countries where corruption has been highlighted. Bolivians elected Evo Morales in part because of his being cleared of corruption charges and his anticorruption platform. As noted, Brazilians forced Collor de Melo from the presidency because of graft in 1992. Twenty years later, their current popular president, Luis Inácio Lula da Silva, will be reelected in 2007 only if citizens believe that he is not personally corrupt. With some 190,000 civil society organizations[22] and a well-developed human rights discourse, Brazilians have established among themselves the foundations of a society in which the rule of law and resistance to graft and other forms corruption may be reaching a critical level, a tipping-point at which the rule of law becomes firmly rooted.[23] Brazilians, especially the Brazilian press, have done well in exposing corruption.

A critical level of intolerance to corruption was reached in the United States only after decades of reform. In a classic popular work, *The Shame of the Cities*,[24] Lincoln Steffens shocked readers with stories of massive corruption in places like Minneapolis, a place some regarded as close to squeaky clean in the late twentieth century. Corruption in the United States continues, as is evident in the indictments or trials of, say, former mayors (Providence, RI; Bridgeport,CT; Waterbury, CT; and Atlanta, GA), governors (George Ryan of Illinois) and legislators (Tom DeLay). However, scandals are not systematic, and they do not roil the nation. When corruption occurs, citizens are comforted that the rule of law is firmly in place. By and large, accountability and transparency function well.

In two series of vivid articles, the *New York Times* and the *Washington Post* painted a picture of Latin America or, in the case of the Post, of Mexico, rife with corruption throughout society, a vice long planted in the culture and rightly causing in Latin Americans a sense of fatalistic acceptance. Much of what was written is true. The articles could have been written any time in the last two hundred years and reprinted with few changes. However, both papers ignore what is being done to combat corruption. Already noted here, but not in the *Times* or the *Post*, is the growing intolerance for presidential corruption. Further, what is emphasized here are the systematic efforts being made by governments, in league with activists from civil society, to fight corruption at many levels. In a word, there is another dynamic, that of anticorruption, transparency, probity, integrity, and ethics that is taking hold in the region and is, in the author's view and that of many informants, noteworthy and, in increasing measure, succeeding. At mid-decade, Latin America shows less corruption than most developing areas of the world.

What, then, is most hopeful to long-term observers of Latin America is not only the changed intolerance to corruption on the part of civil society but also the reforms that accompanied the democratization process. Emphasis has been placed by states and by activists on actions by the state to increase horizontal accountability.[25] The reforms described here are some of the principal ones employed. Privatization was one of the reforms. Under state ownership of firms, public officials involved with these firms had many opportunities to use public resources for private gain. While the occasion of privatization offered an unprecedented opportunity for political insiders to enrich themselves, the process of moving previously state-owned enterprises to private ownership removed a large source of corruption from government hands. These enterprises now had to perform productively, subject to shareholders' evaluations.

Another political reform was extensive decentralization, one of the lesser observed features of democratization, but one of the most important changes. Latin America was plagued by overly-strong central governments.[26] A number of Latin American countries sought to address this imbalance, each in its own way. Tim Campbell of the World Bank contends that, as if by an unseen signal towards the end of the 1980s, many Latin American governments suddenly transferred money and decision-making power to local municipalities.[27] Brazil's president (1995–2002), Fernando Henrique Cardoso, enhanced a movement already in place in Brazil to decentralize governance, devolving power and money to regions and municipalities. He built on innovations written into the 1988 Constitution that established Social Assistance and other Councils. These councils were established at all levels of government to deliberate on policies, such as health, and to monitor their execution. The councils were composed equally of representatives from civil society and the government. Margaret Keck and Rebecca Neaera Abers note the "tremendous numbers of deliberative bodies in which citizens joined with state representatives to discuss problems and make policy recommendations."[28] If the plan was flawed because of the asymmetry of power between office holders and ordinary citizens, Brazil's experience was thought to be worthy of world attention when the United Nations (in 2005) named former president Cardoso as head of its group dealing with civil society.

While one would expect Brazil with one of the largest economies in the world to retool its governance in modernizing fashion, even countries at the bottom are examining and reshaping their governance practices. Bolivia's president (first term: 1993–1997), Gonzalo Sánchez de Lozada, used his own money to create a think tank. The organization concluded that Bolivia's governance had been too elitist, too top-down and suggested that decentralization take place. The Bolivian government enacted the Law of Popular

Participation (1994). This law created smaller units of government and made available greater resources at the local level but was largely derailed by political maneuvering.

A further necessary step, the Law of Decentralization (1995), provided for administrative independence at the local and provincial levels. Bolivia was redefining itself.[29] Anthony Sánchez de Lozada's bold move shifted some power from the central government and placed decisions and financial resources in the hands of local authorities.[30] These two laws were interpreted as being the most ambitious attempt in the region to bring power to the people.

Sánchez de Lozada, a presidential adviser at the time, has argued cogently that large segments of the population in emerging democracies tend to be excluded from the political processes and can be better brought into the processes through decentralization. He also argues that decentralization makes an accountable government in an open society more likely.[31]

Kevin Healy, who has observed Bolivia at the grassroots level for many years as an official of the Inter-American Foundation, believes that while some advances against corruption have been made through Bolivia's decentralization, corruption merely moved to lower levels of governance. In one of the very few empirical studies of decentralization, Mitchell Seligson and associates reported that after the first years of the Bolivian experience only a slight reduction in corruption could be detected. Seligson and Healy both are hopeful that further changes will improve municipal governance. Seligson and others, such as the World Bank, believe that in fifteen years Bolivia transformed itself from a country characterized by centralized control, personalism, and extreme instability into one in which democracy, the market, and decentralization are the chief characteristics. Seligson added that on all three counts, "Bolivia stands in the forefront of trends taking place in the world."[32]

Any help in reducing corruption in Bolivia is sorely needed. Almost half of Bolivians reported they had been victims of corruption.[33] Further, most Bolivians believed that there is more corruption in democracy than under the Banzer military dictatorship in Bolivia.[34]

One of the chief innovations many Latin American countries have made in the struggle for human rights generally and for integrity specifically has been the office of ombudsman, or public protector. This is largely a European creation and does not exist in the United States. In Latin America, the office is often called *defensor del pueblo*. The office deals with citizen complaints against the state.

Most Latin American countries have these defenders of the people.[35] The institution that largely began in 1985 in Guatemala and spread to other countries has been credited with substantially aiding the consolidation of democracy. Ombudsmen supply a need to supervise the performance of government employees with regard to human rights. The office has a wide latitude in investigation, mediation, and education in human rights. Ombudsmen in Bolivia have fostered a dialogue with coca growers and others over the cultivation of coca and the economic development of the Cochabamba region, mediated a major conflict over the use of water, and attempted to halt the notorious October 2003 armed conflict between military and police, among many other efforts. All these events point to a much wider playing field for human rights activity beyond the initial efforts to deter death and torture.

All seven Latin American countries in the initial Public Integrity survey (the number of countries will be greatly increased soon) have ombudsmen. All but Brazil's are rated as very strong or strong. Brazil's ombudsmen are called *ouvidoria*. The office was considered to be too new to be effective. Contrary to many critics, ombudsmen have shown themselves to be strong instruments for human rights protection. In Guatemala, where death squads still exist, the ombudsman often resorts to the press to denounce government irregularities, an act of considerable bravery.

Another area that has become an anticorruption target area for civil society is transparency of and participation in the budget process. A transnational movement has grown up around this aim, the International Budget Project, anchored by FUNDAR in Mexico and by key NGOs in ten other Latin American countries. The project uses budget analysis to advance human rights.[36] Bolivia has also been fortunate to have el Centro de la Democracia (Democracy Center).[37] The center helps citizen groups understand how to effectively participate in the making of public policy, especially in the area of budget policy. In general, the Latin American countries have a poor showing in this area but are making significant progress in the role of legislatures (as contrasted to the dominant role of the executive) in the budget process.[38]

Anticorruption and transparency coalitions constitute a further step toward reducing corruption in Bolivia and elsewhere.[39] One of the countries from which Bolivia's government hoped to learn is El Salvador, where these transparency coalitions have lent strength to isolated efforts. Lastly, empirical research conducted in Latin America since the late 1990s shows there are other practical ways, such as public awareness campaigns, that do reduce corruption.

Fighting Corruption in El Salvador and Honduras

El Salvador is the kind of country where corruption would be endemic and intractable. A civil war left notable divisions; crime rates among the highest in the world and an elitist society dependent on cronyism were elements that could foster corruption. Nonetheless, El Salvador has managed to cast itself into a society where corruption is less common than most of its neighbors. More important, it has put in place mechanisms to control corruption that speak well for its future. It did so through a variety of measures backed up by strong support from sectors of civil society.

First, to describe measures from above, the Salvadoran legislature ratified the Central American Convention Against Money-Laundering and passed in 1998 a national money-laundering law. El Salvador also put in place a more effective and transparent financial management system, anchored by the Court of Accounts. The court has functioned since its creation in 1939 as the highest institution charged with watchdog functions for governmental practices and spending.[40] The court drew a thousand persons from private and public sectors to an event called "Public Management Transparency" in 1999, in a direct attempt to fight corruption by making clear an ethics code for public transactions, such as in government procurement. The Court of Accounts also brought charges against various officials, including several mayors. The International Budget Project noted progress made by El Salvador's legislature in its oversight of the budget process.[41]

The Court of Accounts added an office to receive citizen reports of corruption by public officials. The government also rationalized the organization of its Integrity Office to monitor the financial disclosure activity of public officials. The court itself evolved over time. It was established over two decades ago, but seven persons employed by the court felt compelled to make it a more effective instrument of anticorruption. These persons founded the NGO Probidad, as noted below, to reshape the Court of Accounts.

A major strength for El Salvador has been a network of public agencies and NGOs affiliated with RICOREP, the Network of Institutions Devoted to the Fight Against Corruption and the Promotion of Public Ethics, which was created in 1998 for the region. Within El Salvador the group regularly promotes events related to anticorruption and provides technical assistance. In a word, Salvadorans created a anticorruption and transparency coalition.

Three Salvadoran NGOs that are key parts of this coalition are unusual in Latin America. The Salvadoran Institute for Democracy (ISPADE) made itself part of the regional efforts to educate anticorruption trainers. It implemented programs that included municipal accountability, procurement integrity, and procurement law. The second organization is called the Lima Group. No other country in Latin America, and perhaps the world, has such a group, one comprised of the presidents of the Supreme Court, the National Council of the Judiciary, the First Vice President of the Legislative Assembly, the Court of Accounts, and three representatives from civil society to promote transparency in government. The Lima Group chooses the programs that ISPADE pursues.

Another keystone organization has been Probidad (Probity), an NGO started in 1994 to lobby for the reform of the Court of Accounts. It expanded its activities on a broad front aimed at anticorruption, including television interviews, newspaper articles, and lobbying congressman and public officials. The organization publishes a first-rate anticorruption journal, *Revista Probidad*. Presumably as a result of these efforts, El Salvador has the lowest level of corruption in Central America, with the exception of Costa Rica.

In contrast to El Salvador, neighboring Honduras seemingly has intractable problems in public administration. At the heart of the problem has been the unwillingness or the inability of officials to internalize the need for reform and to put into practice the mechanisms needed to combat corruption.

When Archbishop Cardinal Oscar Rodriguez Maradiaga of Tegucigalpa, the capital, acted as president of the Latin American Bishops (CELAM) from 1995 to 1999, he became convinced that the poor of the region were being adversely affected by corruption. He and other leaders of CELAM carried on face-to-face conversations on poverty with officials of the World Bank and other international organizations. They heard from these officials concerns about corruption, a domestic disease that was eating away public-sector resources and could be diminished. (This was in contrast to external factors over which countries had little control. Latin Americans were turning away from blaming others, as in the dependency debates, to looking at themselves.)

After Rodriguez left the presidency of CELAM, he continued in a key leadership position as chair of CELAM's Commission on Justice and Peace. However, it was primarily in his role as the ranking cleric in Honduras that he carried on a public campaign to call attention to the national evil of governmental corruption and the need to combat it. As always, reform depends on opportunity. One presented itself when hurricane Mitch left sections of the country in devastation, and citizens wondered what happened to large funds generated for disaster assistance. A fair percentage of Hondurans felt that government officials pocketed some of the money. This suspicion thus fueled discussion of corruption as a major national issue.

The government responded to Rodriguez's (and others) lobbying by forming a National Commission on Corruption, but it could not find anyone willing to take the position of chair of the commission. By default, Rodriguez took over the chairmanship of the commission. Rodriguez is much admired by most Hondurans. He was named one of the ten best citizens by a national magazine, despite his acting as the conscience for the country. When the author went to interview Rodriguez at his office, the archbishop (also cardinal) arrived in a Jeep-style vehicle with two SWAT team policemen with automatic weapons and alert bearing. Rodriguez had been receiving death threats. Rodriguez could point to no measurable success of his commission, but he said he would have been content to increase awareness of the problem.[42]

The issue of corruption took center stage in the 2005–2006 Honduran presidential campaign. When Manuel Zelaya took over the presidency in 2006, he made anti-corruption and transparency key targets for his presidency. When sworn in, he signed the Citizens Participation Law, approved by congress the night before, to provide greater transparency of government. If he does act, he can build on notable efforts already underway.

LATIN AMERICA WITHIN A TRANSNATIONAL PERSPECTIVE

National efforts to reduce corruption have been strongly backed up by transnational organizations, ranging from the international bank to international aid efforts of foreign governments, such as USAID. The result caused an unusual ferment of networking in

2006. This can be seen not only in the activities described below but in Respondanet, a website that bills itself as the most complete source of information on anticorruption efforts and is especially helpful for Latin America. A similar network has been provided by Anti-Corrupción Sin Fronteras.[43]

Both governmental and nongovernmental agencies and groups have lined up against corruption. Three relatively new organizations have provided views into the fight that is going on and into progress that has been made. The better known of the three, Transparency International, has gained international renown through increasingly valuable studies and through its trendy index of honesty and corruption, picked up yearly by news sources around the world. Probidad is located in San Salvador and makes its intellectual resources available to other Latin Americans through it website and other means. The Center for Public Integrity in Washington, DC reports on various countries worldwide. Their depictions of individual countries add the perspective of where the region may fit on a worldwide scale.

Older organizations like the World Bank were reluctant to address corruption because of their own limited charters and resources and the sensitivities of member states. However, by 2006 the World Bank had become a major player in anticorruption efforts. The World Bank and regional banks began facing up to the great obstacles to development that corruption posed. While the pressures for reform, as seen in the removals of presidents, have especially come from civil society, reform demands both governmental actions and civil society strategies. To the surprise of many observers, Paul Wolfowitz, upon becoming president of the World Bank, made corruption a major theme of his tenure. The banks and Transparency International since 1992 have built an international coalition to research the magnitude of corruption and to find the best practice solutions.

Transparency International (TI) created a Corruption Index in which most of the nations of the world are ranked on perception of corruption. Some Latin American countries have fared unusually well. Chile has ranked close to the United States and ahead of Spain.

The Corruption Perceptions Index (CPI) reflects a country's propensity to accept bribes according to the perceptions of business people, risk analysts, and the general public. Because of the absence of reliable data, not all the countries of the world are included in the survey. The scores range from 10 (squeaky clean) to zero (highly corrupt). More than two-thirds of the countries surveyed scored less than 5.5, which is the number Transparency International considers the borderline figure distinguishing countries that do and do not have a serious corruption problem. Most Latin American countries fall in the middle range, with only Paraguay near the bottom.

These rankings are based on nonrandom, reputational sampling and are probably less reliable than, say, the Zagat ratings of restaurants in the United States outside of Manhattan where Zagat has less trustworthy appraisals. TI, however, has been an enabling presence for countries to think more systematically about their national corruption problems.

Far more promising as an index has been the recent creation of the Public Integrity Index (PII). This has been intended as a method of gauging how well a country has set itself up to defend public integrity systematically and in many dimensions. The PII measures positive rather than negative aspects, integrity rather than corruption. The focus is on measuring the existence in law and effectiveness in institutions and practices that help to control or reduce corruption, prevent further abuses, and promote effective governance. The approach also has the advantage of pointing out the presence or absence of key anticorruption instruments many Latin American countries have chosen (or not) to employ as a result of demands from human rights groups and others in the private sector. These include whistle-blowing measures, national ombudsmen, anticorruption laws, and anticorruption agencies. The PII will expand to include most of the countries of the world.[44]

The difference between the indexes of TI and CPI can be seen in the case of Mexico. On the CPI, Mexico has advanced a bit to share the 65th (of 158) position, but not enough to shed its image of a widely and deeply corrupt nation. Mexico gets a "moderate" rating in the PII, which tracks corruption, openness, and accountability. By desegregating important facets and substituting institutional mechanisms that are in place rather using reputation, the PII is able to show that Mexico is very strong in electoral and political processes, strong in civil society organizations, and strong in oversight and regulatory mechanisms. (One should note that Mexico has been mostly stymied in its fight against police corruption because of the pressures to abate crime.) In other words, Mexico has built up significant strength from below and from above in its struggle against corruption. That Mexico has made progress in diminishing corruption shows up in publications as diverse as Frommer's *Mexico 2006* and *Foreign Affairs*.[45]

Clearly the fight against corruption is complex, needing to be fought on many fronts. In addition to institutional mechanisms mentioned, open financial accounting by government is essential. Mexico's otherwise rather ineffectual President Vicente Fox did manage to introduce and implement open financial accounting and thereby reduce corruption.

CONCLUSION

If outsiders feel that Latin America is overwhelmed by the "scourge of corruption," it is important to note that larger Latin American countries fall in the middle range of the worldwide corruption scales, that considerable progress has been made, and that mechanisms are in place to make corruption less likely in the future. Much of this has been the result of local, national, and transnational agencies. If globalization brought increased corruption opportunities to Latin America, it also carried with it better practices for combating corruption, tied to an energized civil sector.

NOTES

1. "On the Shame of the Cities," in *Plunkitt of Tammany Hall*, online at Lehrman Center, Yale University.

2. See Keith S. Rosenn and Richard Downes, eds., *Corruption and Political Reform in Brazil: The Impact of Collor's Impeachment* (Coral Gables, FL: North-South Press, 1999).

3. Steve Ellner in "A Tolerance Worn Thin: Corruption in an Age of Austerity," *NACLA Report on the Americas* 27, 3 (Nov.–Dec. 1993): 13–16 explains well the popular pressures that arose in Venezuela.

4. The *London Observer* reported that Pinochet was receiving an annual salary of US $516,000 in 1997, the year before he was picked up in London (Inter Press News Agency, Sept. 14, 2004, online.)

5. S. Bruce Schearer and John Tomlinson, "The Emerging Nature of Civil Society in Latin America and the Caribbean," summary of report for Inter-American Development Bank and conclusions online at synergos.org.

6. Barbara Geddes and Artur Ribeiro Neto, "Institutional Sources of Corruption in Brazil," in Rosenn and Downes, *Corruption:* 21–46.

7. In its 2002 report, Transparency International ranked Costa Rica 40th on a worldwide scale of 102 countries.

8. "Dinero suicio se lava más y mejor en el Norte," Inter-Press Service News Agency, posted online 9/21/2004.

9. Mitchell A. Seligson, "Corruption and Democratization: What Is To Be Done?," *Public Integrity* (Summer 2001): 221–41.

10. Samuel Huntington, *Political Order in Changing Societies* (New Haven, CT: Yale University Press, 1968): 64.

11. Red Anticorrupción Bolivia, "Encuesta nacional de costos de la corrupción para los hogares de Bolivia," (2005, online): 1.

12. Seligson's views were seconded by Latin American bishops. See *America* 191, 11 (Oct. 18, 2004).

13. The Ethical Declaration against Corruption was published in Bogotá: Conferencia Episcopal Latinoamericana, 1997.

14. La Prensa Honduras 1998, online.

15. "Corrupción y conciencia cristiana" (Quito: Conferencia Episcopal Ecuatoriana, 1998; see also Monseñor Vicente Cisneros, "La Iglesia frente a la corrupción," online at probidad.org, April 2002. For a theological statement, see Víctor Manuel García Avalos, "La corrupción en la enseñanza social de la Iglesia," *Revista Teológica Limense* 37, 1 (2003): 31–58.

16. "Carta al pueblo de Dios," (Buenos Aires: Conferencia Episcopal Argentina, 2001).

17. Mario Alberto León, "Propone Iglesia plan para combatir corrupcion," Noticieros Televisa, March 16, 2004.

18. A view from the human rights perspective can be viewed at: www.derechos.org.

19. Mitchell A. Seligson, "The Latin American Public Opinion Project: Corruption Victimization, 2005," *Global Corruption Report 2005* (Transparency International, online): 282–84.

20. Red Anticorrupción Bolivia, "Encuesta nacional": 6.

21. S. Bruce Schearer and John Tomlinson, "The Emerging Nature of Civil Society in Latin America and the Caribbean," study summary of report for Inter-American Development Bank and conclusions online at synergos.org.

22. Some observers believe that a nation needs to be ranked at 5.5 or higher on the Transparency Index before transparency and accountability are firmly established.

23. Lincoln Steffens, *The Shame of the Cities* (New York: Sagamore Press, 1957).

24. See, for example: Scott Mainwaring and Christopher Welma, *Democratic Accountability in Latin America* (New York: Oxford University Press, 2003).

25. Margaret Keck and Rebecca Abers note that strength of government often meant strength of authoritarian control, not strength of democratic institutions.

26. Tim Campbell, *The Quiet Revolution* (Pittsburgh, PA: University of Pittsburgh Press, 2003): passim.

27. Margaret Keck and Rebecca Abers, "Civil Society and State-Building in Latin America," *Latin American Studies Forum* 237, 1 (Winter 2006): 30.

28. Kevin Healy, *Llamas:* 121.

29. Edward Cleary, "New Voice in Religion and Politics," in Edward Cleary and Timothy Steigenga, eds., *Resurgent Voices in Latin America* (New Brunswick, NJ: Rutgers University Press, 2004): 57.

30. Anthony Sánchez de Lozada, "Accountability in the Transition to Democracy," in John Crabtree and Laurence Whitehead, eds., *Towards Democratic Viability: The Bolivian Experience* (New York: Palgrave, 2001): 195.

31. Mitchell A. Seligson, et al., *Democracy Audit Bolivia 2004 Report*, online: 100.

32. Ibid. 175.

33. Seligson, *Democracy:* 187.

34. Chile, Uruguay, and the Dominican Republic do not have ombudsmen, but lobbyists in Chile believe they have made a strong public argument and are close to obtaining an ombudsman for their country.

35. See their guide, *Dignity Counts* (2004).

36. The center is headed by Jim Schultz. See his *The Democracy Owners Manual: A Practical Guide to Changing the World* (New Brunswick, NJ: Rutgers University Press, 1995).

37. International Budget Project, Budget Transparency in Latin America: 2005 Survey, online.

38. Americas' Accountability Anti-Corruption Project.

39. Perhaps the closest equivalent in the United States is the Office of Budget and Management.

40. International Budget Project, Budget Transparency in Latin America: 2005 Survey, online.

41. Interview, Tegucigalpa, Honduras, June 16, 2004.

42. As an indicator of anticorruption activity in Latin America, a principal portal for Latin American Studies, Lanic.org, added in 2005 a major section dealing with transparency and corruption.

43. A relatively new enterprise for indexing the measures taken against corruption is the Index of Opacity. The Kurtzman Group that maintains this index includes fewer countries than Transparency International's index.

44. Enrique Krauze, "Furthering Democracy in Mexico," *Foreign Affairs* 85, 1 (Jan.-Feb. 2006): 58.

Index

About the Author

Edward Cleary is professor of political science and director of Latin American Studies at Providence College. He was president of the Bolivian Institute of Social Study and Action and edited "Estudios Andinos." He is author of *The Struggle for Human Rights in Latin America, Crisis and Change,* and other works.

Also from Kumarian Press . . .

Human Rights and Humanitarianism:

Dealing with Human Rights: Asian and Western Views on the Value of Human Rights
Edited by Martha Meijer

War's Offensive on Women: The Humanitarian Challenge in Bosnia, Kosovo and Afghanistan
Julie Mertus

Human Rights and Development
Peter Uvin

Non-State Actors in the Human Rights Universe
Edited by George Andreopoulos, Zehra Kabasakal Arat and Peter Juviler

New and Forthcoming:

Zones of Peace
Edited by Landon Hancock and Christopher Mitchell

Surrogates of the State: NGOs, Development and Ujamaa in Tanzania
By Michael Jennings

Complex Political Victims
Erica Bouris

Visit Kumarian Press at **www.kpbooks.com** or call **toll-free 800.289.2664** for a complete catalog.

Kumarian Press, Inc.is committed to preserving ancient forests and natural resources. We elected to print *Mobilizing Human Rights In Latin America* on 30% post consumer recycled paper, processed chlorine free. As a result, for this printing, we have saved:

3 Trees (40' tall and 6-8" diameter)
1,199 Gallons of Waste Water
482 Kilowatt Hours of Electricity
132 Pounds of Solid Waste
260 Pounds of Greenhouse Gases

Kumarian Press, Inc. made this paper choice because our printer, Thomson-Shore, Inc., is a member of Green Press Initiative, a nonprofit program dedicated to supporting authors, publishers, and suppliers in their efforts to reduce their use of fiber obtained from endangered forests.

For more information, visit www.greenpressinitiative.org

Kumarian Press, located in Bloomfield, Connecticut, is a forward-looking, scholarly press that promotes active international engagement and an awareness of global connectedness.